Madame Cheryl:

Best Best Wishes!

Ps... Sir Ray
& Lord Joe

Peter at 3 years old.

Peter 60-some years later.

Wok & Roll

Peter House Kwong

My family: back row (left to right) Peter, daughter Melanie, son Justin, granddaughter Ellie, daughter-in-law Stephanie, wife Colleen. Front row: son-in-law Santi, aunt Cindy, uncle Yim (visiting from Hong Kong).

i

Wok & Roll by Peter House Kwong

Copyright © 2018
ISBN 978-0-9982400-8-4

Printed in the USA by Smith Printing Co., LLC
Ramsey, MN 55303   smithprinting.net   1-800-416-9099

Hong Kong Harbor in the 1960s

Hong Kong Harbor today

CONTENTS

FORWARD

FORWARD

It was a bold move, moving from Milwaukee to the North Woods.

My wife and I didn't know a single soul and I couldn't even find St. Croix Falls on the map. It was a total leap of faith, all because of our granddaughter, Ellie. Her family lives in the Cities (took me a while to learn that it is St. Paul and Minneapolis). We saw her maybe three to four hours each time when they came down to Milwaukee for the holidays, and that was it. After the Easter brunch couple of years ago, I told my wife Colleen that we have to move closer to them. Don't want Ellie (her full name is Elise Debra Kwong Wing Yi) who just turned four, to look at me when she turns 18 and have no idea of who I am. The move was most painful, yet it was well worth it.

Elise Debra Kwong Wing Yi

I always wanted to write a memoir/cook book to recap all the fond memories of growing up with food in Hong Kong, with many other fun recipes that I have developed through the years of working with different restaurants. It started out five or six years ago as a retirement project, yet it never got finished. Somehow, it was perfect timing to finish what I started after moving up here. I couldn't handle just sitting at the porch and drink beer all day (tried for a week, but it didn't work). A good friend, who is a retired English professor read my first draft, and her comment was, "Lots of good stuff, but you were here and there and everywhere. You've to tell a story, so readers can follow what you are writing about." Right then, I knew I needed help.

Irene, my good friend and neighbor (another good story) told me about the writing class that she and her husband Robin are attending. Lo and behold, My wife also told me about this same class from one of the libraries that she visited. The good Lord was sending me a message. So I attended this writing class hosted by Carolyn Wedin, called 'Write, Right Now.' I've met so many interesting folks who love to write and to be able to share their inner thoughts, beliefs and experience of life during each meeting. It was fun, educational and spiritual in more ways than one; as every writer is opening his/her own soul, heart and mind, and shares with others their thoughts and feelings.

Sharing your hearts and souls with others? That was a new concept to me. Growing up in Hong Kong, it was not traditional or encouraged to share your emotions and feelings with others. I never kissed or hugged my parents while growing up. You only hear "I love you" in a song or watching a movie. I was elated when I heard stories told by different writers (who are my friends now) about life, their feelings and their passions. To be able to share their dreams and inner thoughts was beyond me.

As fate unfolds, at the class before Thanksgiving two years ago, Carolyn announced that the local paper, Inter-County Leader, to which we contributed an article to each week, was seeking a filler. She was asking her students if we have anything special to contribute. I volunteered. As a chef, I could write something funny but yet practical. It was Thanksgiving, during which a turkey would be on every home's table. To be funny and creative, I wrote an article of how to make Pot Stickers (dumplings) with ground turkey. The recipe is real, and so is my wacky sense of humor. The story/recipe got printed, and another chapter of my life had begun.

I got a call from Gary King, the editor of Leader a few days later. He told me that he enjoyed the article a lot and asked me if I would be interested in writing an article each week for his paper. I was thinking to myself, "What? Writing a weekly column for a paper? Who would be interested? Above all, it would take some time." After much contemplating and consulting with my wife, I told myself, 'why not?' Not only will I be able to improve my train of thoughts, my writing skills, but also I would be able to follow my dreams of completing my cookbook. Then came the next challenge, what should I name the column? I love singing 'rock & roll' with my strolling guitar and I also love to cook. So, why not name the column "Wok & Roll?" Hence, "Wok & Roll" it is. Cooking and rolling along. Ain't that what life is all about? Good gracious, that was 100 columns ago.

Thank you folks who enjoy reading the column. I promise I'll keep writing with whatever comes to my mind – food recipes, funny jokes, my philosophies of life ... and whatever, as long as you're interested.

Thank you all. Or should I say, "Thanks y'all."

Peter's family from Hong Kong. Shown, left to right, back row: Paul, Peter and Francis. Front: mother and father.

My American mom and dad, Joyce and Donald House.

My American siblings (L to R): Robin, Mark, Eric, Lori, Leesa, Fred and I.

EDITOR'S NOTE

Peter has become one of the most popular columnists to appear in our newspapers in just his first few years of writing. His recipes, humor and honest portrayals of life's adventures make this book a great read. A few comments from his readers:

"I look forward every week to Wok and Roll. I love Mr. Kwong's sense of humor and I've tried most of the recipes. Sometimes I cut and paste the columns and send them to my children to read and try."

"He is so entertaining - it's good to have a world view of food here in the North Woods."

Due to comments like that I encouraged Peter to assemble his weekly columns into book form, not only to introduce his work to a new audience but to create a keepsake for his loyal fans.

It's been an honor to help Peter create this book, which I feel is inspirational in itself when you consider the road he traveled and hard work he put in to realize the American dream.

Copies of "Wok & Roll" will no doubt be passed around among circles of friends, not just for the recipes but for the great warmth, humor and wisdom Peter offers in these pages.
- *Gary King*

CHAPTER ONE: FRIENDS & NEIGHBORS

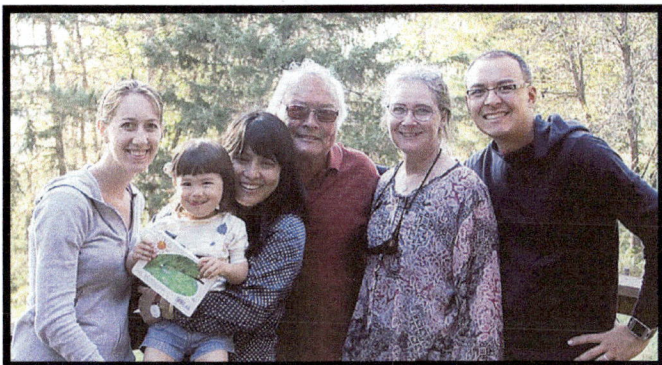

Family in 2015 at new home in North Woods.

Finding friends was easy

My biggest fear in moving to the North Woods from Milwaukee was not knowing anybody. We lived in the neighborhood of Milwaukee for 13-plus years and we hardly knew any of our neighbors. The first time we struck a conversation with the neighbors across the street was on the day that we were moving out. Lo and behold, we have more friends now than we ever had; in the short two years that we have lived here. We've met so many great folks that we consider friends in such a short period. We're very fortunate indeed. The good Lord has been kind to us since the move. It is really a blessing indeed.

I've met 20-some barbershop brothers since I joined the Indianhead Chorus. The cooking classes that I taught have many new students whom I am still trying to match their faces with their names. Then, our friendly neighbors. First it was Irene and Robin across the lake; and then Paul and Janet down the street from us. My wife and I are beyond words. How come the folks up here are so warm and friendly and so accommodating? Whatever the reason, we are totally enjoying the hospitality of the local folks. Most grateful indeed.

We met Paul and Janet from the Petal Pusher, down the road, the summer that we moved in.

My wife was planning to have a garden at the front yard and was looking for different ideas. We followed the tiny green signs on the roadside that led to their home. My word, we were totally taken aback by the beauty of their garden. There were different colors of gorgeous flowers, with different plants with names that I didn't know. We introduced ourselves to the owners, Janet and Paul Supplee, and we just hit it off immediately.

Paul is a pastry chef and I am in the culinary business; we started to talk shop, just to find out that he has more award-winning medals than I. My wife, Colleen, loves flowers and plants, so she and Janet started chatting. Later, Paul revealed that he is also a potter, owning a studio named Bog House Pottery. Colleen is a potter too, besides being a painter and jeweler. Don't remember how long we were there, but we left with our car loaded with flowers and plants. I think I paid for some of them and the rest were housewarming gifts. Goodness, we hardly knew those folks.

Colleen started to tell me why their flowers/plants are different than those in the nursery/market. They are cheaper and healthier. Don't know much about plants, but the word 'cheaper' sounds wonderful. Then she started to tell me that Janet has a passion about what she does, and she loves to share her knowledge with anyone and everyone. She actually dug out the plants from her yard to sell them to strangers, hoping that they would find a good home. She would plant a mother plant, just being able to give/sell the baby plants. Colleen was so excited about the plants that we were going to have in our garden – hepatica, trillium, bloodroot, wild ginger, jack in a pulpit ... all Greek to me.

It was interesting to find out that besides all the medals that Paul won, he also worked in the White House during the Clinton administration. Oh my! He was trained in

Switzerland in the '80s and a graduate of CIA. No, not the spy agency, but the culinary institute. Being a pastry chef, you've got to be creative, love working with your hands, and enjoy baking. That's why he is a potter too. He makes all kinds of pottery – coffee cups, birdhouses, water pitchers, just about anything. There is a certain trace in his artwork with his signature on it; yet every piece is different. I can relate to that. Even though I created the recipes for my students, I never cook the same meal twice. All depends on the ingredients that I have, and what mood I am in. Paul told me that baking is an art as well as a science. You would follow the procedures, yet each batch is always unpredictable. One thing that hits me, he said, "I do what I like, I don't worry about what other people think." Is that a statement from a true artist? I play piano and sing with my guitar. When I sing, I just close my eyes and sing what I feel and how I feel, couldn't care less of what the audience thinks of me. Never knew that baking can be of the same principle.

Being in the corporate world all these years, Paul found his freedom and passion in doing his own thing. Same with me,

I enjoy teaching cooking classes, doing something I enjoyed in my past life. I was a chef, a restaurant consultant and an adjunct professor. But now, I can combine all those passions in just being a cooking instructor.

Paul loves to play chess, and so do I. We have had our friendly battles. This is indeed a great game. How else would you be smiling, seeing your opponent being destroyed and on his knees? We still remain friends. Amazing.

Where have all the flowers gone? Go to their yards and find out.

Our new home

Can't believe that it has been over a year since we moved to the North Woods. It has been a welcome change and I have been keeping myself busy with writing, singing and teaching cooking classes in different communities. Living in Milwaukee, driving 15 to 20 minutes was a long haul. Now, driving an hour or two just to get to my destination is considered "normal." How life has changed and it all starts from wanting to be closer to our granddaughter in Minneapolis. It pays off, as before the move, we saw Elise (or Ellie) two to three times a year and only for two to three hours each time. Now, we see her two to three times a month! We're still counting our blessings.

We love our new home. Not knowing anything about the North Woods, nor knowing anyone in the community, moving here was a big risk indeed. And somehow, everything works out just fine. The sun rises each morning from our front porch, and sets in the evening at our back porch. Growing up in Hong Kong and living in different big cities through all these times, I never had the experience to be so close to nature – listening to the rustling trees, the tweeting birds, the giggling squirrels and the geese squawking loudly above. Never knew that I could actually listen to the wind blowing. It is totally amazing.

I had my knee replacement surgery last November and the recovery is painful but reassuring. Still can't run or ride my bike yet but I am capable to walk up and down the stairs without holding on to the railings. I was told that walking is the best therapy. And so I've tried to walk as much as I can each day. Then my wife got me this little tiny timer, a Fitbit, to measure how many steps I actually walked. Ahhhhh! To start out, 5,000 steps a day is required. So, the first day, I walked and walked and I clocked in 12,000 steps! But I paid the price the next day, having to sit with the heat pad on my back for hours. But that's the price you pay to stay healthy, no!?

It is quite pleasant to walk in our neighborhood, as we live close by the Ahlgren Wildlife Preserve. There are lagoons, creeks, ponds, and miles and miles of shrubs and trees. I never realized that there are so many different kinds of wildflowers around. And the different species of birds! I wanted to write more about my walking venture, then I came across a message that my wife wrote on her weekly newsletter to her congregation. I was so touched, as it says everything that I wanted to say. So I asked her if I can quote her article, and she said, "Sure, if you would take me out to dinner." There is a McDonald's in town, so what the heck. And here is what she wrote:

"While canoeing through the marshes, streams and lakes near my home, I am aware of the richness and the quantity of plants and creatures that populate the neighborhood.

"One evening during sunset this week, my son and I paddled quietly to the edge of the marsh and sat silently, watching the usually elusive sora (small marsh bird) feeding on the insects and snails as they walked gingerly on the lily pads. As we sat and watched the sora, we became aware of a brown head poking up through the water munching loudly on a lily pad – a beaver had surfaced to have a snack.

"We recognized the blessing of being a part of such a rich environment. Clear, clean water flowing through the marsh; deep silt nourishing and providing a foundation for the lilies and other marsh plants; crustaceans, tiny plants and fish providing sustenance for the birds and mammals. This is an environment so clean that frogs and dragonflies abound and one can see the bottom of the lake between the waving water plants.

We recognize our responsibility to keep it clean and healthy for the next generations of plants, animals, and our own children and grandchildren. What if we created all of our homes and neighborhoods with the care we see reflected in the beauty of the wild, natural world? What if everyone who enters our homes and our workplaces feels nourished and supported by the surroundings and the way they are regarded by the people present?

"As people of faith, we are called to create beauty and nourishment for all those around us. We are named 'Apostles' that will speak of Christ in the way that we interact with others. The statements that we make through our words and actions invite others to be who God calls them to be, as well. Imagine a world of healing and health, of beauty and brilliance, and a world that praises God through its very being."

Well, I couldn't have said it better. I am just counting my blessings over and over, to be able to enjoy nature in the most heartwarming way. My wife has taught me a lot in observing what is around me, not just taking big steps to get to my destinations. I have started to notice the spiderwebs filled with morning dews, glistening under the sun; the tracks that are left by the night-traveling animals; the various shades of greens composed by different trees, grasses, shrubs and wildflowers. Oh my, how come I have never noticed them before?

I guess I should scratch McDonald's and take her to someplace different. Hmmm, there is a Dairy Queen close by.

Write Right Now

I joined Carolyn's Write Right Now class shortly after we moved here from Milwaukee. That was one of my biggest fears living in the North Woods. First, I got lost easy, even with the GPS on. And the winding roads at nighttime with no streetlights are big challenges for a city boy like me. Took me a while to find out that Luck and Frederic are north of us, Turtle Lake is on the east, Taylors Falls is on the west and River Falls is south of us. It took me almost six months just to establish where we live. And then the next big fear – "What now, brown cow?" I didn't know one single soul up here, what to do? What to do? But a new life has begun.

I joined the local barbershop group, the Indianhead Chorus, and instantly, I have 20 new friends who share my passion for singing. We had no ideas about the town we live in – where is the post office, the police department, the library and the hospital? Things we took for granted, but needed so desperately in our daily life. We went to the visitor center and met a lovely lady, who shares the same name as my wife, Colleen! It is an unusual name, but somehow, there are lots of Colleens living up here (at least there are two in Menards).

Carolyn Wedin (seated, right) hosted members of her class for a feast.

We asked her a lot of questions, and she patiently gave us all the detailed information. My wife loves to read, and she had book club gatherings almost every week when we lived in Milwaukee. So, when she popped the last question as we departed, "Do you know of any book clubs around here?" Colleen smiled back, and said, "Yes, we do. As a matter of fact, I'm with a group right now. We've been together for many, many years. I'll call you to let you know when our next meeting date is."

She did call, and lo and behold, we joined her book club with four other wonderful couples. And that's not the end of my story. My wife loves bird-watching. And at any place – library, farmers market and banks, someone would tell her that she should meet this Robin guy, who is an expert in wildlife. For months, she had been searching for this Robin the Bird Man. And do you believe that he is the husband of Irene, the friendly neighbor who came to our house to introduce herself? After she heard that my goal of retirement is to write a cookbook, not just a cookbook about recipes and stuff, but a memoir about my life living in Hong Kong in the '50s, she said, "Peter, you should come to our writing class and learn more about writing skills. Robin and I belong to this writing group called 'Write Right Now,' you can meet more people who share your interests. And who knows, maybe you'll learn something you find interesting to complete your cookbook." There are two classes offered, one in Frederic, and one in Luck. Out of curiosity, I signed up for both classes. And holy smoke, what great folks I encountered.

I read an article in the Writers' Carousel by Angie Lunden, a new participant of the group, a few weeks ago. I couldn't help but smile, and told myself, "Ha, she is writing about me too." Carolyn's group is totally unique. Even though she is in charge of each meeting, you do not feel her dominance. Everyone has a chance to read what he/she writes; and afterward, all participants have a chance to air what they think about the content. She never says, "No, that's not good," or "No, you didn't get your point across." She simply smiles and says, "Hmm, just what would you do differently so your message is clearer?" I sat in front of a group of professional writers, as many of them had already published their own books! I shared the agony of Angie. It does take some courage to join the group. But no regrets! None whatsoever!

I love to write, but being in the restaurant business all these years, all I wrote was recipes, portion and styling, training manuals, operation manuals and business plans. Effective, yet boring materials that you read before you go to bed, so you can fall asleep faster. I started to write this book "Cook with your Heart" many years ago. It is not just about cooking and recipes, but about the lifestyle around food while I was growing up in Hong Kong. There had been many tries, but somehow, I wasn't happy with them at all. I finally have the courage to put what I've written so far and stapled them together to form a book. And I had the courage to show it to Carolyn for her comments. She summarized the book as "Good, but can you do better?" And she told me what I needed to work on. It was a rude awakening. I was writing about my story, my perceptions, and my experience. And I did not get the message out to the readers, so they can share same. Just like my cooking and singing, writing is about sharing your passion and feelings with others, so in turn, they can share whatever you are offering.

So, I decided to get rid of what I've written, and started again from scratch. Writing the weekly column has helped me out tremendously. My wife, who is an expert in English writing, is big help. She helps edit my weekly column just to make sure that I don't embarrass the readers with my grammar or punctuation. I'm proud to say that my errors are fewer and fewer these days.

So, my dear friends, if you have a desire to write and share your passion of your ideas and philosophies with others, come join Carolyn's Write Right Now class. It is fun. And how else can you meet new people who are just like you? I'm glad I joined, and give thanks to Carolyn, and all the dear friends that I've met. Yes, I ain't worried about meeting new friends these days. But I still have to figure out if I should turn left or right to go to Balsam Lake. Ahhh, life of chances.

Barbershop singing

Besides cooking, I enjoy singing. I love cooking because it gives me the opportunity to be creative and it gives me such joy and pleasure when my guests enjoy every bite. I was testing my new recipe of General Tso's chicken a few weeks ago and I asked my neighbors and friends to be my guinea pigs (literally). The neighbors brought their 4-year-old and 10-year-old grandkids along. Watching the young ones finish their plates and ask for more was priceless. I was in heaven!

My wife and I used to sing in the nursing homes in Milwaukee, and again, it was such a joy entertaining the seniors. A lot of them were in wheelchairs; however, they would be tapping their toes or moving their fingers to the rhythm of our songs. Oh, we could sing to them forever.

My first encounter with barbershop singing was when I was a kid in Hong Kong. There was this promotion video that all theaters used when Disneyland first opened in Southern California, showing the Pirates of the Caribbean, the Matterhorn Ride, and the Jungle River Ride. Somehow I was more intrigued by the barbershop quartet singers performing on the Main Street. Four different guys singing four different parts, yet together, they formed such a beautiful harmony. How was that possible? I didn't remember Mickey Mouse or Snow White, but the image of those four guys just would not go away. And, by chance, I joined the Big Chicken Chorus when we lived in Atlanta, Ga. I kept with the barbershop singing while living in Milwaukee, and finally, I joined the Indianhead Chorus here.

I've been singing barbershop on-and-off for almost 20 years. Yes, it is a hobby all right but so is stamp collecting. Where else can you find 20 to 30 guys who share the same interest as you, show up week after week, and spend a few hours learning and practicing great songs together? No, we do not get paid for what we do - we do it because we all enjoy the camaraderie and the harmony we create. There are four parts to the chorus, the lead, the bass, the tenor and the baritone. The lead sings the melody, the bass sings the low parts and the tenor sings the high notes. The baritone picks up notes that nobody carries and those notes sound strange and odd indeed by themselves. Hence, the baritones are always the butt of all jokes that they can't carry a tune. But in reality, without those baritone brothers, we'll all be flat. Get it? B flat?

We were taught to excel and exceed in whatever we do to become successful in life. Yet, barbershop teaches me that the best results come not from just one person's effort, but the whole chorus performing together, with each person carrying his part to become one voice.

Starting out in 1938 in America, now the society has turned global. I was in Toronto attending a wedding, and the groom's family was from England. The groom's father and I were having a friendly conversation during the rehearsal reception. I was trying hard to keep up with my long lost British accent (I was born in Hong Kong, a British colony then). I found out that he also sings barbershop. So, we sang a couple of Pole Cat songs, which are songs that all barbershop singers learn before they can become an official member. The guests were mesmerized. How could two strangers who have never met make music together? It was a magical moment indeed.

Everything is magical in barbershop. It is fun, educational, entertaining and most rewarding. Yes, it is free, but it also comes with a price – your passion, your dedication, and your drive to give the best of what you can for yourself, and for others. There would be 30 singers singing, yet you only hear one voice. Most amazing indeed.

And here is more information about our chorus from our Marketing Director Ken: The Indianhead Barbershop Chorus started making music over 58 years ago. It is a fraternity of about 30 men drawn together by a love of singing four-part acapella harmony music.

The chorus is a chapter of the Barbershop Harmony Society. The members come from Burnett, Polk, Barron and St. Croix counties in Wisconsin, and a few come from Minnesota. Members come from many backgrounds and all drawn together by a love of singing and fellowship.

We sing at Music in the Park, churches, and various community festivals. Many of our guys regularly sing out as members of quartets.

11

My Scandinavian friends

Our mentor of the Writer's Carousel, Carolyn Wedin, just had a season-ending gathering with all the writers getting together to celebrate another successful season. What a joyous occasion indeed.

I volunteered to make the meal for the occasion with the help of my trustworthy buddies. It was a crew of six: Phil and Joanne, Robin and Irene, Geezer Bob and Nanette. What a fun time it was ... at least, for me. We cranked out six courses in two hours.

Yes, six courses. Do you believe it? Not one of which was peanut butter and jelly sandwiches, folks. They were mouthwatering entrees, and our guests all claimed that they were much better than the restaurants that they visited. Well, after a glass or two of wine, everything tasted great. We cranked out a feast for 20-plus more guests within two hours. Unbelievable, you might say. No, I say, we had great sous chefs and everyone knew what they were supposed to do. It was like singing in a chorus, when everyone knows their part and could chime in at any given moment, what joy it was. All I did was bark orders:

"Dinner is served at 4 p.m. and this is 2:45 p.m. So, move, folks. Chop, chop." Obediently, they all moved accordingly without any resentment or questioning my authority. Oh, how I love that. I never got that at home.

Our six-course meal consisted of:

• Bruschetta, pronounced "Bros/ka/ta." I got my head bit off one time from my Italian colleague when I said 'Bro-she-ta, so, for your health, learn how to say Bros/ka/ta and live a longer life.

• Garlic toast with fresh minced garlic

• Pork piccata with capers and fresh lemon juice

• Chicken cacciatore with tomato sauce and a lot of wine

• Ensalada Italiana with black olives, hard salami and tons of cheeses

• Fettucini Alfredo with fresh cream and more cheeses

So, we divided the team with different tasks. Right when

our guests showed up at 4 p.m. the meal was ready to be served. Everyone was amazed. How could it be done? Well, how could our grandmas do it year after year, serving us all these great meals single-handedly? It's planning and executing. Grandma did it all by her lonesome self. As far as I know, Grandpa's job was to stick his head in the kitchen every half an hour, and yell, "How much longer for dinner? I'm hungry."

Well, I want to share with you the team effort of Phil and Geezer Bob, as their garlic toast was a hit. I always judge the success of the meal by looking at the leftovers. There were only two pieces left out of the 30 or more that they made.

Most restaurants' garlic toast is toasted bread sprinkled with garlic powder with Spanish paprika on top, and that is it. Well, this garlic toast takes a little bit of work, but it is absolutely delicious. Here is the recipe:

Garlic toast, serves four:
- 1 loaf Italian or French bread
- 1 cup garlic, minced
- 1/2 pound. butter
- 1 cup Italian parsley
- 1 cup of three cheeses, shredded
- Paprika to sprinkle on top

Method:
Turn oven on to 375 degrees. Slice the bread at an angle, 1/2-inch thick. Layer the bread evenly on a baking sheet pan. In a saute pan, heat up the butter and then add minced garlic. Cook until brown, then spoon the butter/garlic mix onto each piece of bread. Use a brush to make sure that the bread is coated evenly. Put in oven for 10 to 15 minutes until nicely brown and toasted. Remove from oven, then generously add the three-cheese blend on top, and put back in oven again for another 5-10 minutes. When cheese is melted, remove from oven, sprinkle with paprika and add a small pinch of Italian parsley on top. Viola! It is great just to serve as is, with a glass of wine or complementing any entree.

A gathering of writers for an Italian feast. Shown, left to right, Irene Bugge, Geezer Bob, Joann and Phil Peterson.

The happy chefs.

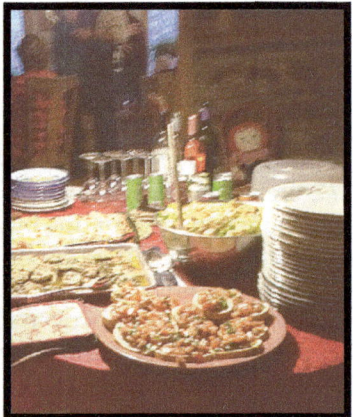

Italiano fiesta.

While everyone enjoyed the rest of the dinner, it is this special dessert that I want to share with you all. It is called Blotkake for Syttende Mai (cream cake for the 17th of May or for birthdays, etc.). It was beyond words. I am diabetic and I don't like sweets, but this cream cake is beyond words. It is a very popular dessert in Norway and the cake is decorated to look like the Norwegian flag. Here is the recipe:

Blotkake for Syttende Mai:
- 8 large eggs
- 1 cup sugar
- 1/2 cup flour, sifted
- 2 cups fresh/frozen raspberries or strawberries
- 1-1/2 pints whipping cream
- 3 tablespoons powdered sugar

Method:

Preheat oven to 350 degrees. Line a rectangular 9-inch by 13-inch cake pan with parchment paper. Secure the corner by adding a dab of butter in each corner.

Beat eggs and sugar until stiff, about 10 minutes. Gradually fold in the sifted flour, mixing by hand. Pour mixture into pan. Bake at 350 degrees for about 30 minutes. Turn the oven off but leave cake sit for two minutes before taking it out. Loosen the cake and flip it upside down on a cooling rack. Let it cool completely. Slice the cake horizontally in half. Place the bottom layer on a serving platter. Spread a layer of fruit mix on top. Whip the cream with added powdered sugar till stiff, then spread over the bottom layer. Place the other layer on top, and repeat with fruit mix and whipped cream. Decorate the cake to look like a Norwegian flag, or just enjoy it the way it is.

Anyway, it is December and I haven't cranked up my snowblower yet. Maybe another mild winter ahead of us? Let's keep our fingers crossed.

I teach different cooking classes, Chinese 101 and 102, Mexican 101 and 102, and Italian 101 and 102. I have yet to cook any Scandinavian cuisine. Maybe it is time to learn. Is lutefisk a Scandinavian specialty? Maybe it is not time yet.

One of Peter's cooking classes

Cooking classes

Before we moved up to the North Woods, I was busy working as an adjunct professor at a culinary school (BTW, do you know the difference of a regular professor and an adjunct professor? One class. Yes, one class. A regular professor has 6 classes, with all the benefits. Yet, an adjunct professor would only get 5 classes, with NO benefits; however, all job responsibilities are the same), a chef doing cooking demonstrations, a restaurant consultant, and singing with the local barbershop. Yes, I kept a busy life; thinking that I would retire after moving up here; and just sat at the porch and drink beer all day. A great concept indeed, but it only lasted a week. Story of my life, can't sit still and not doing anything. However, not knowing anyone, and not knowing where the job opportunities were, I just sat and waited. Then one day, there was a knock on my door.

My wife is a pastor, and she was looking for a church that she could belong to. We tried different churches in the area, but nothing hits home. Then, remembering her good friends Rebecca and Bob who live in River Falls, she decided to give their church a try. They used to live in Milwaukee, and we visited each other often. Then one day, they decided to move up north to be closer to their granddaughter. They absolutely loved it. So we decided to follow their footsteps, and we ended up loving it too.

After the service, there was a gathering at the dining hall, and we were so honored as the whole congregation greeted us and bid us welcome. Many questions were asked - 'where do we move from?', 'why the move?', 'what did I do before the move?', 'what do I do with my spare time?'...... I gladly answered all the inquiries politely, not thinking much about them afterwards. However, a call came from Monique Squire, the director, a few days later, asking me if I would be interested in teaching a cooking class for their community education program in River Falls. My first thought was, Holy Smoke, River Falls is an hour south of where we live. As I've no sense of directions, it took me a while to get my bearings down – east of us is Turtle Lake, south of us is New Richmond, west is Taylor Falls, and Frederic and Luck are up north. Don't remember how many times I passed our house without recognizing it. Hence, my mail box is nailed with reflectors of different colors. Can't miss it anymore!

So, after much contemplating, I decided to give it a shot, what the heck; it is better than sitting at home. Never realized that my new career has just begun. I think I taught Chinese 101 to begin with. After the class, the students were asked to fill an evaluation form. Rate from 1 to 5, some students gave me a 6, others an 8, and one even gave me a 10! Needless to say, Monique was elated. Little did I know that she is also the head director of the Northwest region of Wisconsin. A lot of calls came afterwards after she told her other directors about me. A lot of calls came from different districts afterwards – Frederic, Luck, Amery, Unity, St. Croix Falls, Osceola, Rice Lake, and Spooner…., I became a local celebrity chef overnight.

Life is a hoot!

The art of eating

Do you remember when was the last time your family ate together, with no interruptions from phone calls or texting messages? I thought it was a joke at first, when a friend sent me an email, attaching a picture of a family having dinner together, and each family member (except the baby) was on the cell phone, either receiving or sending text messages. I was quite sad after finding out that it wasn't a joke after all, but is actually happening in our daily households these days. What happens to the good old tradition, with everyone sitting around the dinner table? We passed the food, ate the food, and then talked about our days at work or at school. We would spend hours at the table, no TV, no kids from next door visiting, just time for the family. And then, all of a sudden, the tradition is gone; what happened?

As our standards of living keep rising, the need for more disposable income also escalates. The days of parents staying home and taking care of all the household chores are gone. Now, most parents have to carry a full time job, plus taking care of all the household chores! And guess what happens to the family meals and eating together? Yes, times have changed, and life has changed with time. We see the long line in the drive-through at the fast food joints, folks can't wait to get their food, so they just chow down quickly in their cars on their ways to the movies or the malls. All of a sudden, I remember the comedian George Carlin's famous 'Words of Wisdom' – "We've learned how to make a living but not a life", "These are the times of fast foods and indigestion."

We spend thousands of dollars signing up for weight watching programs in order to lose weight, and watching "The Big Loser", wishing that whatever works for those 'winners' would also work for us. However, I have two words of advice that would resolve most of the issues. That is, "Eat slowly". We have totally forgotten the art of eating. 'Slow eating' is not only an art, but it is also a health requirement. When we fill up our stomach with foods and drinks, the message that we are getting full doesn't reach our brain for at least twenty minutes. Yes, twenty minutes. So, when we are wolfing down our dinner, and our stomach tells us that it has reached capacity, just where do you think the food that we consume in the extra twenty minutes are stored?

There are many ways/styles to serve foods in different restaurants:

French – table side service, the server would finish cooking your meal and serve next to your table, most often in a cart. Expect a lot of spectacular 'en flammes' entrees when the server actually sets your food on fire by heating up some brandy (or cognac)!

Russian – the server(s) will carry plates of food around the table, and you just pick out what you want. Or, it can be in a buffet form. But still, you got your choice.

English – plates or bowls of food will be set on the table, and the guests will just pass each item around. I think we have adopted that style with our Thanksgiving or Christmas Dinners.

American – each plate is already plated in the kitchen. Your entrée usually consists of meat, starch and vegetables. Soup or salad and desserts are extras.

Chinese – either all the entrees are set on the table; or they are served separately, one course at a time.

Regardless what style to serve the food, they all emphasize the 'togetherness' in enjoying the food, and the time it requires to relish each meal. Eating is an event indeed, not a necessity of just filling the stomach with whatever we can conveniently track down.

So, what is "the Art of Eating"? Here are some simple rules to follow:

Take the time to eat your food, allow 15 minutes for a quick breakfast, half an hour for lunch, and at least forty-five minutes for dinner. Actually sit down and eat your food slowly.

Can you taste your food? Instead of filling your stomach with whatever you can get your hands on, chew slowly so you can taste what the ingredients are.

Don't forget the '20 minute rule'. It takes 20 minutes to send the signal from your stomach to your brain that you are full.

When your brain gets the signal, stop eating. Take whatever is leftover home or refrigerate it for later.

Exercise, or engage in activities that will get rid of those excess calories.

Focus on eating and spending time with your family. Turn off your cell phones. Rediscover the pleasantness of being with family and friends.

It is simple and healthy. Start eating slowly and enjoy the food. Try it, you'll love it.

Whole steamed fish

Foods that dare you to try

Growing up in Hong Kong, I ate many things that were common in the daily diet but are considered barbaric here in the States. However, after studying about foods that folks eat from different parts of the world, I find out that we are all from the same pot.

Some people eat whatever just to survive while others eat bizarre foods just to be adventurous. Living in the 21st century in America, we are indeed spoiled. The older generations still remember eating all parts of an animal after you slaughtered it at the farm. But the only way our younger generation sees an animal organ these days is probably at the laboratory at school.

Frozen octopus

21

There are four must-have delicacies at any Chinese banquet: abalone, sea cucumber, fish stomach and shark's fin. A few centuries ago, during the Qing Dynasty, other delicacies included camel's hump, bear's paw and monkey's brain. It is something like the scene from "Indiana Jones," but the monkey was alive! I don't want to go into details, but eating something that is still alive revolts me, even if it is considered a delicacy.

I love seafood. In Korea and Japan, they have a dish called sannakji, which is a sashimi, raw fish, made with live octopus. They pick out the octopus from the tank, cut off its tentacles and clean it out while you are watching. After they add some sesame oil and seasoning, they serve you the plate with the tentacles still moving.

Folks are warned to chew their food properly, as the "live" tentacles can get stuck at your throat and literally choke you to death.

Oh, poetic justice!

Another one is called ikizukuri, which is another sashimi dish that some Western countries have banned. The chef would take a live fish from the tank and carefully slice off the meat, piece by piece, while the fish is still alive. Then, after the plate is beautifully decorated and served, the chef puts the skeleton back into the tank. Not knowing that it is without any flesh left, the fish actually swims around for another three to four minutes. I do not have the nerve to watch the video again.

While I admire chef Andy Zimmern, or known as Zimmerman in some shows, who dares to eat anything in any country he travels to, there is one thing that he admits that he can't eat. That's stinky tofu. It is soybean cake, tofu, that has been fermented for two to three weeks and then deep-fried. Whenever the vendor showed up in my neighborhood with his stalls, the whole street smelled like a sewer overflow. But folks would line up to get their share, actually happily paying for them. Another stinky fruit that is banned from hotels and airlines is durian. Though many adore it and claim that it is indeed "the king of all fruits," most others would hold their nose and quicken their steps when noticing a durian is being cracked open nearby.

My mother loves the thousand-year-old egg, but I have never developed an appetite for it. These duck eggs are covered in clay that is mixed with ash, salt, quicklime and rice hull, and buried. When they are unearthed, the whites have turned into a grayish gel, and the yolk is solid black. My mother would slice them lengthwise and eat them with pickled ginger slices. Ugh! And how about balut, a favorite in southeast Asia and in some parts of China. It is the embryo of chicken before it is hatched. You can still see the form of the chicken, with beak and all, and you just steam them and then eat them or cook them with wine. Supposedly great for women after childbirth. Double ugh!

While I heard of Rocky Mountain oysters, or prairie oysters, I never knew that they are bull testicles. But in China, ox penis is indeed a delicacy. I have seen a picture of a chef holding the dish, a large dish indeed. All I can say is, "Oh my goodness." Guess I have been in America too long. And just how do you eat the darn thing?

A lot of countries treat insects as a delicacy, tarantulas, locusts and grasshoppers. I did try some water cockroaches in Hong Kong. They were black, shiny and oily, and smelly too.

You peel off the wings, which were the tough part, and you suck out the soft innards and chew on those tiny hairy legs. Don't remember how old I was then. I guess you are entitled to do dumb things when you are young.

While the Russians have their caviar, fish eggs, the Mexicans have their escamoles, ant larvae from the agave plants. Agave is what they use to make tequila. I was told that the larvae are quite delicious, have yet to try ... someday soon, with a lot of tequila as chaser, of course. Then, when in Hong Kong, I did try some rice worms that were steamed with eggs. They were found in rice stalks amongst the rice fields. If I recall, I did have more than one helping. They were banned in Hong Kong, but my father had some special connection with the owner.

I did like to munch on the fish eyeballs when I was a kid, but seeing how the Japanese eat the tuna eyeball makes me think twice. They were sold in the market in small packages. They stare at you like a huge camera lens. Don't know where to start if I have to eat one.

Just when I thought I have tried everything, I have encountered lutefisk here in northwestern Wisconsin. Maybe we should talk about that some other time.

For a semiretired guy, I can't believe just how busy I'm getting. I expected to sit on the porch, sipping tea or beer, depending on what time of the day it is, and watch the sunrise or sunset. Does beer go with sunrise or sunset? Still deciding. But I was dealt a different deck of cards. In my boardroom game of "retirement," there is no block for actual sitting around and doing nothing. The rule is that I have to go round and round the block till I can't breathe or move a muscle, and on the board that's called total exhaustion. But I can't complain. I rather be doing something productive than sitting around eating bonbons.

As you know, I am teaching cooking classes – Chinese, Mexican and Italian. Long story how a Chinese guy ended up teaching Mexican and Italian cuisine, but that's what life is all about; it is just full of surprises. Anyway, I was showing the students in my Chinese 102 class how to make egg drop soup.

After I showed them the simple procedures, they tasted it and said, "Wow." And then almost in unison, they exclaimed, "You mean that's it? That's all you have to do to make this delicious soup?" What do you want me to say? Good things in life do not have to be difficult and complicated. So, let me share with you what I did. Talk about warming your heart on a cold evening, and it takes less than 10 minutes to make.

Egg drop (flower) soup for four
    1 tablespoon chicken bouillon
    1/2 cup rice wine (sherry)
    4 eggs, scrambled
    1 stalk celery, diced
    6 mushrooms, diced
In a pot, heat 2 quarts of water. When boiling, add 1 tablespoon of chicken bouillon, or simply use 2 quarts of chicken stock that comes in a box. Add sherry, diced celery

and mushrooms. Mix 1 tablespoon of cornstarch with 2 tablespoons of cold water. Add to boiling stock and mix gently. When stock thickens up a bit, slowly pour in the scrambled eggs. Then turn the heat off immediately. Cover with lid to let the steam keep on working. Place in separate bowls and sprinkle some shredded scallions on top with a couple drops of sesame oil. Viola!

Note: So that the eggs will form a floral pattern, the added cornstarch mix is a must.

Chicken corn soup for four
1 can creamed corn
1 can whole-kernel corn
1/2 cup sherry
4 eggs, scrambled
1 tablespoon chicken bouillon
4 oz. cooked chicken, diced

In a pot, heat up the cans of creamed corn and whole-kernel corn, and add one can of water. When the water boils, add sherry, cooked diced chicken and chicken bouillon. Then add 1 tablespoon of cornstarch mix. When soup thickens, drip the eggs slowly into the soup. Cover with lid and let it steam for a minute or two. Top with sesame oil. And here is your chicken corn soup.

When I was growing up, this was my favorite soup. We ordered it every time when my family went out for dinner. My brother and I would be smiling when we were eating it. And the restaurant owner would look at us and smile too because the soup cost is low and he would make more profit than with any other entrees.

Cream of tomato soup
A good friend has a late harvest of tomatoes. This is October, and he still has tons of tomatoes clinging on the vines. He has 46 plants in his yard. And if each has six tomatoes hanging on it, Lordy, there would be 276 tomatoes available! "Would you like some garden-fresh tomatoes?" my dear friend asked. "But of course," I said, knowing that the market is charging $1.68 per pound for some tomatoes

flown in from Mexico. How could anyone resist the chance of getting fresh tomatoes from the garden? He brought over two large bags, which weighed over 10 pounds, if not more. He smiled, and said, "Thank you, have at it." He was actually thanking me with a smile, instead of me gratefully thanking him. Kind of makes me suspicious of his motives.

Regardless, looking at these two huge bags of tomatoes, the question I asked myself was, "What now, brown cow?" I can eat one or two tomatoes a day. Sprinkled with a little bit of salt and pepper, they are wonderful. But 10 pounds! My Lord, it will be spring when I get to the last one. And I'm sure that they won't be as fresh as they are now. Hmm, what to do, what to do? Then I thought about this old recipe, cream of tomato soup. That's it, cream of tomato soup it is. Growing up in Hong Kong, eating a westernized meal was a venture of its own. We used chopsticks with our meals. But, in a western restaurant, you used forks, spoons and knives. How quaint!

And tomatoes were imported, as the Chinese farmers had never heard of such an animal. They would slice the tomatoes paper thin, and put them on top of a salad or something. I was tickled pink when I bit into a piece of tomato then. But now, what can I do with 10 pounds of them?

Aha! Why not make a tomato bisque, a rich, thick tomato soup? So, I got out my Cuisinart, cut the tops off the tomatoes and just pureed them. Yes, all of them. And in a large pot, I would saute some garlic first, then just add the puree with some chicken bouillon. Then I would add some cornstarch mix to thicken the stock, and then a handful of cheeses – mozzarella, cheddar, parmesan – and a pint of half and half or some evaporated milk. The soup should be rich and thick.

Season it with salt and pepper, and serve it hot with garlic toast or crackers. And of course, with a glass of Cabernet Sauvignon, what else could be better? So, who cares if it is snowing outside?

You are what you eat

How many of us are "on a diet" these days? I crack up when I notice that someone who is on a diet, and supposed to be eating something healthy and nutritious, are actually ruining their health by eating something labeled "healthy alternatives." Sugar is bad for you, right? So they switch to artificial sweeteners. And guess what's in those tiny packages? You guessed it - chemicals that are made with artificial ingredients. How about margarine? If you think that butter is bad for you, how about eating a large spoonful of "flavored" petroleum? If you really like fruit juices, squeeze your own. I started to read the food labels just to justify my opinions on what I'm writing about and I am appalled that, after two to three ingredients that are actually related to the label, the rest are all chemical ingredients that I do not recognize, or have names that I can't even pronounce.

So, what can we do? What is safe to eat? Actually, all foods are good for us, but only in moderation. I love pizza and fried chicken, but can you imagine eating them five or six times a week, with bread sticks or mashed potatoes with gravy on the side, and then wash them down with two or three local brews, or Diet Pepsi or Diet Coke? And how about those snacks before and after the meal? The potato chips, M&Ms, chocolate cookies, ice cream ... aah, all my favorites! And talk about moderation. The French are known for their tasty cuisine, wines and desserts. How do those ladies stay so trim and skinny? The key is moderation, something that we can all learn. Instead of feasting on candy bars, just have a piece of great chocolate. Instead of a huge steak or fish, have an 8-oz. piece with vegetables on the side, and one piece of great bread instead of eating a whole loaf with dinner.

We just happen to be the most obese country in the world. Yes, in the whole wide world. How can that be, when we have all these diet and health programs to help us stay trim and fit? I think that it is all our own fault – we are the land of plenty and abundance. We are what we eat, but there's no one there to tell us when, and what, we can or cannot eat anymore. There are no more moms and grandmas who love us and tell us what to do. We are independent and we are free, so we can do what we want, and eat what and whenever we want. And guess what happens? Oh, we do miss our moms and grandmas.

Well, enough lecturing. It is Chinese New Year, eat and drink and be merry, but all in moderation. Let's be healthy and stay healthy. Believe it or not, with health, wealth will be right behind.

Now, let's talk about the food that we eat during the Chinese New Year. The Chinese are very traditional (I dare not say superstitious) and we will eat anything that will bring us good fortune and prosperity. So, what's there to eat? What's on the menu on a New Year's banquet? Here are the key ingredients. And restaurants would create fancy names to enhance luck, joy and happiness.

• Lettuce – pronounced as "sahn choy," which rhymes with words meaning generate fortune. Who doesn't want fortune knocking on your door?

• Dried oysters – pronounced "hoa xi," which rhymes with prosperous market. A must for those who invest in the stock markets.

• Dried sea urchin, or dried sea cucumber – pronounced "hi zin", which means open heart, or totally delighted or absolute happiness.

• Fish – pronounced "yu," which rhymes with leftovers. Every household prefers having leftovers in their bank accounts than being in debt, right? We always serve the fish whole, with the head and the tail. Whatever relationship we are in, we always finish what we started with. That's most important in careers and businesses.

• Shrimp – pronounced "ha." The sound we make when we laugh, a joyous sound in our household.

• Broccoli – pronounced "jei lan," which rhymes with get rid of hardships. "No more hard times henceforth," my mother would say when she dished me spoonful of broccoli into my rice bowl.

• Pork tongue – pronounced "chu lei." Lei rhymes with profit. Be profitable.

So, what a way to start a new year with a few of these easy to make dishes:

- Broccoli with Shrimp Cantonese.
- Steamed whole fish with wilted lettuce in oyster sauce.
- Pot stickers with dipping sauce.

Remember that pot stickers resemble a stuffed wallet or purse? Hope your new year will be filled with laughter and no hardships. You will generate a great fortune with a lot of leftover profits.

Kung hey fat choy! Happy Year of the monkey!

Wok and roll with MSG?

Yes, I know that there's a connection somewhere, but somehow it irks me when I hear people say, "Oh, I can't eat Chinese food. It gives me a headache and makes me ill."

Well, as much as I don't like that statement, there is certainly some truth to it. No, eating Chinese food won't give you the headache, but it is the MSG that is added to the food that does. Yes, a lot of folks are sensitive to monosodium glutamate, myself included. The Food and Drug Administration has classified MSG as a food ingredient that's "generally recognized as safe.", but its use remains controversial. For this reason, when MSG is added to food, the FDA requires that it be listed on the label. As a matter of fact, we can find MSG (sold as accent) in the market place. So, out of curiosity I checked out all the foods in our household; snacks, soups, salad dressings and package seasonings. Lo and behold, there is MSG in each and every one of them. Then I conclude that MSG, like sugar and salt, is not bad for you when used in the right proportion. However, a lot of restaurants want to reduce their production costs therefore instead of using expensive herbs, spices and extensive cooking procedures to make the food tasty, they just add a spoonful of MSG instead. It is bad business and it is a lose-lose situation, as when guests get sick, they simply won't return again.

MSG is a food enhancer invented by a Japanese food scientist during the WWII era. It is an extract made from seaweed and vegetables. MSG itself has no flavors, but food that is laced with MSG somehow does taste better. It is a trick that MSG plays with our brains. On the back of our tongues, there are thousands of pores that let the brain know how the food tastes. When contacted by MSG, all the pores open up and we enjoy the fullest flavors of all five senses – sweet, sour, bitter, umami and salty. And mmm, everything tastes great.

However, when we're done with the meal, those pores close up, and at the same time withdraw the water content from different tissues around the area; that's when the troubles begin. First, I've got to drink gallons of water (or pots of tea), as my throat just went dry; second, I've developed a slight headache; and third, I've begun to sweat. But those symptoms happen only when I eat at certain restaurants.

For many years, researchers have found very little connection between MSG and the sickness it causes:

- Headache
- Sweating
- Nausea
- Chest pain

The largest MSG manufacturer Aji-No-Moto actually is here in the states. These days, instead of making them from extracts of seaweeds, they are made from corn glucose that is put through the same fermentation process, which is similar to the one used to make yogurt, beer and soya sauce.

No, Aji-No-Moto did not pay me to endorse their products (even though they should), but I just want to clear the statement that, "Chinese food gives you headaches and makes you sick." And even if the chef uses a small amount of MSG to enhance the flavors of their dishes, it is perfectly OK. It's those places that use tons of MSG to create the flavors that cause all the problems. Come to think of it, how can those buffet restaurants that charge $5.95 to $6.95 for "all you can eat" survive? And the price also includes your beverage and desserts! How do they even make a profit? You get the answers right, buy cheaper products and make them taste great by adding tons of MSG. You pay little and get plenty in return. Everybody is happy!

Next time when you open a bag of BBQ-flavored potato chips and find out that the more you eat, the more you want to go for a beer or a soda, think twice, my dear friends.

Chow mein or lo mein?

A good friend asked me if I have any good lo mein recipes, as his family loves those crispy noodles with vegetables. "Oh, you mean chow mein," I thought out loud, not intending to embarrass him. After all, mein is mein - who cares as long as they are delicious? Yes, "mein" means noodles in Chinese. There are many kinds of noodles but the most popular ones are made with wheat flour, or flour with egg. The other popular one is made with rice, which is called "mei fun." Chow mein noodles are the crunchy ones, they are fried till the noodles are crisp and then the toppings are added to the top. Lo mein noodles are soft, which just come out from boiling water and then are mixed with shredded vegetables and sauces. Then there are noodles with soup. Shanghai noodles and won ton noodles fall into that category.

In Chinese, "chow" means stir-fry or fried. And "lo" simply means mix. The noodles used can be of any kind: flour noodles, egg noodles or Japanese/Korean-style udon noodles. Most noodles are manufactured in factories, they mix the ingredients, flour and water, sometimes with eggs added, in huge mixing bowls. Then the dough is flattened and sliced by a cutting machine, some are packaged and sold as fresh noodles in the market while others are dried first and then packaged separately. Those would have a longer shelf life. Most noodles are long strands that can be stretched over 10' or more, how they fold those long noodles in a small package is most interesting. For that reason, at most banquets honoring someone's birthday, one of the main courses is "longevity noodles," which may be served with soup or just stir-fried. The noodles served symbolize long life. It is fascinating watching the server divide a big bowl of noodle soup amongst 10 or 12 guests. His left hand is equipped with a ladle, while the right hand holds a pair of long bamboo chop sticks; he fills the ladle first with as much of the noodles as he can and then skillfully cuts the strands with his chopsticks. He then goes around the table to serve everyone. It always amazes me that, no matter how many guests there are, there is always enough noodles for everyone.

There are many versions of chow mein. A lot of restaurants would put a bed of crispy fried noodles on the plate first and then add the stir-fried ingredients on top. I've seen a restaurant that actually used fried egg roll wrapper strips as crispy noodles and that works well. So now the question remains ... what do you prefer? I have come up with a simple recipe for each. So, try them and then you can decide.

Chicken chow mein, serves four
Ingredients:
• Chicken, 1 lb. cut in strips and marinated with 1 tbs. cornstarch, sesame oil, sherry and soya sauce, "the four S's."
• Remember this: 1 tablespoon of each of the four S's for 1 pound of meat.
• Vegetables: julienned zucchini, carrots, bean sprouts, broccoli and cabbage, 4 oz. of each.
• Noodles: 1 lb. dry flour noodle or egg noodle.
• Sauces: 1 tsp. black bean sauce; 2 tbs. oyster sauce; 1 tbs. sesame oil; 1/2 cup wine (add 1 glass for chef).

Method:
First, cook the noodles in a big pot of boiling water, as you would for cooking spaghetti. Take out noodles when they are al dente, which translates to "to the tooth," meaning soft but has a bite to it. Drain well, set aside and wait until the noodles are completely dry.

Second, in a heated wok, add 1 cup of oil. Fry the noodles, browning each side until it turns golden and crispy. Take them out and put on some paper towels to absorb the extra grease.

Third, leave wok with 1 tbs. of oil, add 1 tsp. black bean sauce and cook chicken strips until done. Remove chicken and add vegetable mix to wok. Cook for two to three minutes, add the cooked chicken, add 2 tbs. oyster sauce and top with sesame oil for extra aroma.

On a large platter, put fried crispy noodle at the bottom and pour the stir-fried chicken mix on top. That's it. If you prefer more sauces, add a half cup of wine at the final stage. Rather than slicing and dicing vegetables, I just use a couple of packages of slaw mix to save time - they are already julienned carrots, broccoli stems with some red cabbages. If you are like me and like your foods colorful with exotic flavors, add shitake mushrooms or, if you like it spicy, add a tsp. of chili paste to your sauce. Again, you are the master, add whatever ingredients fancy you and your guests. Remember the golden rule: your food should look good, smell good and taste good.

Chicken lo mein

This is more simple. We can skip frying the noodles and just follow the rest of the procedures:
- Cut the chicken in strips and marinate with the four S's.
- Boil and drain the noodles.
- Cook the chicken strips until done.
- Remove the chicken and cook the vegetables.
- Add chicken, noodles and mix well with the vegetables.
- Mix well, add a half cup of wine to make it more "saucy," and don't forget the glass of wine for the chef.
- Adjust the flavors with more oyster sauce.
- Add 1 tsp. of chili paste for a spicy kick.

Whatever mein you are going to try, it is going to be delicious. After all, it is fun and easy to make, and it is tasty for the whole family. Enjoy.

Foods that go extreme

Just when I thought that I grew up eating foods that are extraordinary and different (you can say weird if you want) in Hong Kong – steamed cow brain, chicken embryo, shark fin soup, bird's nest stew ... etc., etc. – here in the States, folks are trying to create foods that will make your hair stand on end, in the name of "fashionable" and "trendy."

On the way to the West Coast a few weeks back, I read an article in the complimentary magazine about what stadiums are offering to the crowd these days to attract more fans. In Atlanta, when the Braves record is the worst in the big leagues (or close to being the worst), the executives are finding new ways to get the fans excited and have a reason to show up for the games. I lived in Atlanta for three years, but I don't remember how much we paid for tickets then. But the memory of the Brewers game is still fresh. Tickets are between $35 and $55 for average seats (first level), and parking is $7. Beers and brats are $6 each. So, it would cost over $100 for my wife and I to attend a game. It was worth it if they played well and won. But, it was a different story footing over $100 just to watch them get smashed. It was demoralizing.

Years ago, the Dodger Dog was most famous. The stadium would be serving the foot-long hot dog that was "loaded," and it was available only at the stadium during the game. But now, the term 'loaded' can be used loosely, especially at the Braves ballpark. Somehow, they came up with a T.E.D. – The Everything Dog. Funny, that's the name of the former owner, Ted Turner. Hope that's a compliment. Don't know how I would feel to have a wiener named after me. Anyway, T.E.D. has everything under the sun. Starting out with a pretzel bun, there is a foot-long hot dog, all beef, in the center. Then, layered with french fries, jalapenos, cheese, chili, BBQ sauce (Coca-Cola-infused), tortilla chips. And are you ready? It is sprinkled with popcorn. I saw the picture, and my first reaction was, "Oh my Lord, how am I going to eat it?" No mouth is big enough to swallow the first bite! (Well, there are always exceptions). Yet, they charge $15 for this monster, and it is going wild. Despite the Braves losing streak, fans would drive to the stadium for a bite of T.E.D. Again, I hope that it is a compliment.

Other stadiums, noticing the success of T.E.D., are coming up with their own creations, trying to outdo each other. Nutrition value? Who cares? Well, in Texas, where everything is huge and big, comes "Wicked Pig" from the Texas Rangers Globe Life Park. This double-decker sandwich costs $27, and is made with bacon, pulled pork, sausage, prosciutto, sliced ham, coleslaw, pork rinds, and topped with BBQ sauce. It is totally obscene and insane. But when the public goes wild, more outlandish items pop up: Atlanta's Burgerizza, a $26 pizza sandwiched between a 20-ounce beef patty with cheese and the works. And Kansas City's Champions Alley Dog, a $15 bacon-wrapped, deep-fried, foot-long frank that's covered and draped on a pretzel bun. And Pittsburgh's Cracker Jack and Mac Dog; yes, hot dog, Cracker Jacks and mac and cheese in a bun with caramel sauce and deep-fried jalapenos - all for $11. (Doctor's bill, $350; but who cares?)

Aha, while you are savoring all these exciting concepts, more are popping up. Love it ... human imagination has no boundary. And try this for size – Kaboom Kabob, that's a 2-foot-long skewer threaded through chunks of chicken and vegetables. And the Tanaco, a 2-foot-long taco. Only in Texas? At this point, yes, but it can be anywhere. I once knew about a restaurant in Wisconsin that serves a 10-pound burger. Actually it is in Sheboygan, a small town 20 miles north of Milwaukee. I thought I heard it wrong at first when a friend told me that's their specialty. A 10-pound burger? Who can eat it? You must be crazy or insane! As much as it is a gimmick for the owner, the price of the burger is $28; but for whoever can finish the whole burger, it is free! And they will take a picture of you and post it on their "Wall of Fame." I've no desire to be famous, yet I've deep admiration for the few whose pictures reflect their determination and appetite. In straight translation, a 10-pound burger means 40 quarter-pound burgers in one sitting. How can it be possible, eating 40 burgers in one setting? But, there are pictures on the wall, proving that they are the true heroes indeed. I remember my favorite movie, "Cool Hand Luke," when he ate all the hard-boiled eggs in order to win a bet. But these guys ate a 10-pound burger just because they wanted to, and they enjoyed it, bet or no bet. I heard that there are steakhouses in Texas that would do same, that if their customers can eat an 8-pound (8 pounds, not 8 ounces) steak, they can have it free! Holy smoke, that's 128 ounces of meat. I once did a study for a buffet restaurant, that your stomach can only hold 36 ounces of food and liquid. That's how the restaurants figure how much food they need to prepare, and hence, their profits. If everyone can wolf down an 8-pound steak, plus side dishes and drinks, they'll go broke in no time flat.

Ahh, life is too short. Enjoy life and eat and drink and be merry. What's the point of filling our stomach just because? I miss the Brewers, and I don't mind paying $100 to watch them play. Maybe they'll win for a change. If not, maybe adding some popcorn to my brats with no extra charge, just because?

Restaurant with no name

Most of the restaurants would have big signs in front of their eateries, some even with flashing lights to catch your attention. Yet, there's one restaurant that has no name at all. McDonald's has its big "M" Golden Arches; Pizza Hut with its Red Roof; and we all recognize Domino's when their delivery car drives by flaunting its rooftop sign. So, what restaurant has no name in the front? Give up? There would be three letters, KFC, with a portrait of a smiling elderly gentleman. You got it – Col. Sanders Kentucky Fried Chicken. Driving down the freeway, we know that there's a McDonald's close by when we see the big Golden Arches. What marketing genius indeed. KFC has a portrait that stands for scrumptious, delicious and "finger lickin' good" fried chicken. How can it be possible? How do we make connections with a smiling gentleman and his famous fried chicken?

I have been in the hospitality industry for years. I've seen a lot of restaurants come to fame with a simple concept. I have also seen a lot of restaurants that went down the hill. According to the Small Business Administration, 95 percent of restaurants fail in the first year. Do you believe that? That's why, while most bankers want to loan you money, (that's how they make a living; bakers sell breads and cakes; butchers sell meat; and bankers sell money); when they hear the word "restaurant," they smile and then kindly show you the door.

I first encountered KFC when I came here to the States 40-plus years ago. We have fried chicken in the Orient, but it is totally different here. In the Orient, we would hang the chicken to dry for a day or two, then brush it with honey, then slowly pour hot oil over the chicken till the skin turns crispy, and the meat would be moist and tender. Yet, Sanders called for a different recipe. He would season the chicken with his 11 "secret" herbs and spices, coat them with a cream mixture, then deep-fry them. Outside is crunchy and crispy, yet the meat is tender and favorable. How can it be possible?

Harland David Sanders was born in Indiana. Even though he did serve in the military, his title of "Colonel" was dubbed to him by the governor, as his famous chicken was bringing in a lot of awareness to the state of Kentucky. His dad passed when he was young. Harland worked a lot of odd jobs to help his mother sustain the family. He loved cooking and had developed this 11 secret herbs and spices to fry his favorite chicken dish. His career started out on the side building of a gas station, his fried chicken got more and more popular and he then had to move to bigger places to accommodate the growing business. In 1935, when he was 45 years old, he knew that he had to bring his business to another level. It took a long time to fry the chicken in a regular fryer, so he started to fry them in a pressure cooker. It worked! The cooking time was cut in half. So, Harland was carrying his cooker and his 11 secret herbs and spices and traveling around the country, looking for a financier who would back him up with this new concept. Thousands had turned him down and more would laugh and taunt him, "Selling just fried chicken and nothing else? You'll go bankrupt in no time flat!" He would still be wearing his bright white suit and his black bow tie whenever he went; his trademark - an old man with goatee, selling fried chicken. What a joke. Finally, Pete Harman from Salt Lake City, Utah, loved his fried chicken, believed in his passion and dream, and became his partner. Indeed, the last laugh came later when he sold the concept in 1964 for $2 million. That is a lot of cash now. Can you imagine that amount 50 years ago?

His 11 herbs and spices recipes had been guarded for many years. Even though the company has changed hands many times, that was the sacred guarded recipe. But somehow, like the song "Secret Love," the secret is not a secret any more. Recently, the Chicago Tribune has published the recipes found by the nephew of Col. Sanders' second wife. So, folks, are you ready to make your own famous fried chicken?

Here is the "secret" recipe that feeds four:
Ingredients:
- 1 chicken, quartered
- 2 cups flour
- 2/3 T salt
- 1/2 T dried thyme
- 1/2 T dried basil
- 1/3 T dried marjoram
- 1 T celery salt
- 1 T ground black pepper
- 1 T dry mustard
- 4 T bell pepper powder
- 2 T garlic salt
- 1 T ground ginger
- 3 T ground white pepper
- 1 cup low-fat cream
- 1 beaten egg
- 4 cups canola oil

Directions:
- In one bowl, mix all spices and flour together.
- In a second bowl, mix cream and egg.
- Soak the chicken pieces in the wet mix and coat with the dry mix.
- Heat up oil to 350 degrees and fry the chicken pieces for 10-12 minutes, then set aside to cool.
- Fry the chicken at 350 degrees again for 15-18 minutes till golden brown; turn over only once.
- Cover a plate with paper towel to absorb the extra oil and lay the chicken pieces on top.
- Enjoy.

Please note that, depending on the equipment you have, results may vary. Experiment with it until you get it exactly the way you wanted.

When I returned to Hong Kong around 1975, I saw a lot of Kentucky Fried Chicken stores all over the island. But then, there wasn't a lot of business, as folks weren't used to Westernized fried chicken served with side dishes like coleslaw and mashed potatoes with gravy. I was told that the concept didn't make it and finally closed down. However, when my wife and I visited Hong Kong and China a few years ago, there were KFCs everywhere but this time, they served congee, a porridge or a rice soup, with fried rice instead. How clever! You have to be persistent and know your market.
Hats off to the colonel. He would be smiling at all of us licking our fingers.

CHAPTER THREE: FOOD

The joy of sharing

For some strange reasons, I've been very popular with the students of the middle schools lately. First, I was invited to speak at the Osceola Middle School students on Career Day. Then I was invited to do a cooking demo at Luck Middle School during their Asian week. Out of nowhere, Spooner asked me to do an after-school program for their middle school students. It is nice to be around all these young souls. One of the students, don't remember which school, called me "Uncle Chef Peter." Now, if that doesn't melt your heart!

I talked to 60-70 students in Osceola Middle School. It was fun. Thank goodness for my volunteer work in my younger days. For many years, I was a volunteer for the Junior Achievement program, talking to younger students about business ethics, career paths and how to start a business of your own. The class is usually 25 to 35 students, all young and mostly eager. Some of them couldn't give a hoot what I was talking about, all they cared about was how their hair looked and where they were going to hang out on weekends. While most would really pay attention to my every word.

I never got used to speaking in public, or in private, for that matter. English is my second language, and I try not to embarrass myself as much as possible. After many years, I still had an accent, especially when I got excited. I would blabber off and everyone would look at me, and go, "huh." (Yes, that included my lovely wife.) As a favor to an old friend, I decided to become a Junior Achievement volunteer, and share my "wisdom" with those young kids. I was much prepared for the challenge but it was a still a semi-disaster. Never been good in public speaking. I stuttered in front of 30-some young kids staring at me. My throat went dry and I was sweating even though the AC was going full blast. Thank goodness nobody laughed, and they were kind enough to give me a standing ovation afterward. The experience really helped me out in building my confidence. Now I can speak in front of a small or large group, talking and demonstrating at the same time, without missing a beat. I guess doing something nice for others always comes back later to benefit you.

Doing a cooking demo for Luck Middle School is a different story. Karl Wicklund is the director of my barbershop chorus, and his wife works at the Osceola Middle School where I did my Career Day talk. I do a cooking class at Frederic Middle School and his brother works there, too. His associate whom he works with is the husband of Mary Miller, the community education director at Frederic. It is really freaking me out, as everybody knows everybody around here, and everyone is related somehow. I can't go anywhere without someone telling me that one of their relatives/friends/neighbors/associates knows me. Never in my wildest dreams did I think that I would gain such popularity. I absolutely love every moment. Come to think of it, living in Milwaukee for 14 years, the only time our neighbors across the street came to say hi was on the day we were moving out.

Anyway, when Karl asked me to do a cooking demo for the kids, I thought it might be 10-20 kids, no problems ... It was 60-70 kids. What a surprise! As I mentioned, cooking for one and cooking for 100 is the same amount of work – you have to plan the menu, buy the food, prep it, cook it and then clean up. Luckily I got help, and quality help, I should say. Found out that two of the instructors took my cooking classes before. Boy, were they a big help. Once the stations were set up, it was simple. We made Crab Rangoon with dipping sauce. I am going to share with you how simple it is and the fun we had. Ready?

Ingredients: (for 12)

Wonton Wrappers	1 package (24)
Sea legs	8-oz. package
Cream cheese	1 8-oz. package

Dipping Sauce:

Orange marmalade	1 12-oz. jar
Crushed pineapple	1 12-oz. can

Methods:

Mix sea legs and cream cheese by hand, that's our mix.

Mix marmalade and pineapple well, that's our dipping sauce. Spice it up with some hot sauce if desired. Create your own profile.

Lay wonton wrappers on counter (make sure it is clean). Brush the edges with egg wash first, put 1/2 teaspoon of sea leg mix in center, fold it over, making sure that the edge is sealed so it won't burst when fried. If desired, crimp the edges for a fancier look.

Heat up wok/pot and fry at medium heat, with 2" of oil. Serve immediately, while they are hot (toasted). Easy and simple indeed. You can make a big bunch of these and freeze them for later use.

I didn't realize what the after-school program is till I got involved with Spooner. It is a program designed to help the kids after school so they have a place to stay till their parents get home (if they do at all). Some of the kids live in homes that have no heat, no electricity, or if they have a home at all. My goodness, this is America, how can it be possible? I looked at those kids, the nicest, cutest, most courteous kids I've ever known. They said, "thank you" and "please" with the friendliest smiles. Above all, they love my food. I taught them how to make chicken enchiladas, and they all wanted more after seconds. So, here is the simple recipe that you can make at home:

Ingredients: (for 12)

Shredded chicken	24 oz.	*(get it from a cooked rotisserie chicken)*
Cheese	12 oz.	
Corn tortillas	24 (2 each)	
Cilantro	2 cups	
Onions	2 cups chopped	
Tomatoes	2 cups chopped	
Green chiles	2 cups	
Enchilada sauce	1 large can	

Methods:

Open the can of enchilada sauce and pour in a bowl. Dip the tortilla in the sauce and set on a platter, add chicken and cheese, and tomatoes and onions if you like. Roll it up gently and put seam side down on a baking dish. Fill the dish and then top it with leftover sauce. Sprinkle with cheese and bake in oven at 375 degrees for 20-plus minutes or till cheese is melted and browned. Sprinkle with cilantro and served with sour cream on top. Maybe with some sliced black olives – use your imagination.

Something to warm your stomach and melt your heart.

Wok and roll with hot pot

Hot pot dinner is one of my most favorite. Now that the weather is getting cold(er), it is time! What makes cooking hot pot exciting is not just about the gathering and feasting, but it is an event indeed:

• Who shall we invite? Anyone who loves company and enjoys fun conversations and great food.

• How much food do we need? More than needed, as always. In general, one can consume 36 oz. of food and beverage (of course, there are exceptions). The leftover stock makes the best soups for days to come.

• How to accommodate the settings with plates and plates of food? Prepare everything beforehand and stack them in the refrigerator. Then bring them out to the counter, and then to the table two to three platters at a time. With the hot pot in the middle and all the setting and dipping sauces, the space is quite limited. There is a strategy to the madness in how to orchestrate the "flow" of colors, flavors and aromas. In general, meat goes first, then vegetables, then seafood, and then noodles and tofu ... etc., etc. You're the master of the ceremony. Fan everything nicely on the platter. The eyes will be feasting first.

Everyone has his own setup - a sauce dish, soup spoon, pair of chopsticks, and a small wire basket with long handle to cook stuff that can easily slip away. And everyone creates his own dipping sauce - a blend of soy sauce, chili paste, sesame oil, chili oil, add minced garlic or shredded ginger and scallions. Make sure that all the foods are sliced into very thin bite-size pieces, 1-1/2" long by 1/4" thick, so they will be cooked within seconds in the hot pot.

• Sliced meats: beef, chicken, pork, lamb, liver, etc.

• Seafood: shrimp, crab claws, oysters, clams, fish fillets, etc.

• Appetizers: fish balls, beef balls, beef tendon balls, fried and fresh tofu.

• Vegetables: napa cabbage, spinach, scallions, chives, oyster mushrooms, etc.

• Others: noodles, rice sticks, vermicelli, udon (Japanese noodles), etc.

In hot pot dinner, there is no etiquette to observe, just enjoy the fun and the company. You should have a little respect for others, such as never picking up any food that you did not drop in the pot. If you find a piece of "hidden treasure" floating around, ask before you consume it.

Remember the "mis en place" (list of ingredients)? Take out your pad and pencil, and let's walk through the whole process:

• The cooking pot. Actually we just need a burner and a boiling pot of soup (use chicken consume). Do not use a pot that is too deep, as your food will sink to the bottom and disappear fast. There are many kinds of burners:

• Electric: that's the easy one, just plug it in.

• Gas burner: uses small can of butane, very efficient.

• The authentic brass boiler: featured only in movies and expensive restaurants. Has a tall chimney in the center with a trough around to hold the soup. Uses real wood, do not never use charcoal. It is deadly!

• Chairs are optional: it is comfortable, yet after a while, you would be eating standing up.

• Food goes down faster.

• It is easier to watch for your food that you drop in the pot, making sure that no one "borrowed" them by mistake.

• The food: as mentioned earlier, most folks can consume 36 oz. of food and beverage. So, if you have 4 oz. each of nine items that you'll be serving, the guests will be full. If you have eight guests, I would purchase 32 oz. (8 x 4 oz.), or 2 lbs. of each kind of meat. And same formula with other ingredients. And folks can also eat more, as the dinner can stretch out to three to four hours.

• Any kind of beers and wines will be great. Make sure you stock plenty. And for the nonalcohol drinkers, jasmine tea is a must.

Don't forget to stage your dinner in courses - put the meat in the soup first, then vegetables, meatballs and last - all the noodles to soak up the flavors. Eat slowly and take your time between courses. Make sure you have extra soup prepped, as you might have to keep adding more soup to the pot while it keeps boiling.

So, it might be minus 15 F outside, but no one would ever notice! Trust me on that. Enjoy!

One tomato, two tomatoes, three tomatoes, four

It's spring. Glad we survived our first "fearsome" winter. We purchased an oversized snowblower after we heard horror stories of being buried in 10 to 15 feet of snow. But we only used the snowblower three times. I am not complaining. And now, my wife wants to plant her own garden. Needless to say, first thing she did was to call our dear friends and neighbors Robin and Irene for advice. "How to start your own vegetable garden here? And what to do to have a variety of tomatoes?" she asked. Not only does Robin know birds and animals, he also knows plants and vegetables. So, he brought leftover fences from his own garden with a bunch of different tomato starters. And now, we have our first garden, gopher and deer proofed. I can see the tiny shoots from the snow peas and the tomatoes sprouting already. Hmmm, can't wait.

I love tomatoes. I once read a sign put out by my colleague in the culinary school:

"Knowledge is to know that tomato is a fruit, wisdom is to not put them in your fruit salad."

So, tomato is not a vegetable, I didn't know that either. I love tomatoes because I just love the texture and the flavor. It is said that they are also good for:

• Warding off cancer – lung and stomach, diabetes and atherosclerosis
• Preventing heart disease
• Protecting against thrombosis (blood clots in the blood vessels)
• Warding off inflammation

What a wonderful fruit indeed! However, unless you grow your own, most of the tomatoes we get here are imported from Mexico or someplace south. They are good, but can't ever compare with any homegrown tomatoes. And then, Irene and Robin came over one day with a box of cherry tomatoes and said excitedly," Here Peter, try this." I popped one in my mouth, and went, "Oh wow," and I kept doing that till I realized that I needed to save a few for my wife. She tried one, and said, "Oh wow." So we asked Irene where they got them, and why are they so different. I will let her tell her story (look for it in the Writers' Carousel). But I am totally amazed that they are actually locally grown here in Milltown at Endeavors. We took a tour there, and I was dumbfounded to see that there are ripe tomatoes hanging on the vine, ready to be picked and consumed. Most imported tomatoes are picked when they are green and have to go through different stages, six to be exact, before they turn the marketable red that we see in the market. The stages are:

- Green – color of a head of lettuce
- Breakers – the green color is slowly fading
- Turning – starting to turn pinkish
- Pink – from light pink to a dark pink
- Light red – becomes a pinkish red
- Red – bright red and shiny

All the processes are being monitored and controlled in a heated warehouse. Just how natural is that? And one thing that impressed me the most is that those folks at Endeavors hired employees with disabilities to work in their plant. Looking at pictures of the workers holding up flowers and vegetables that they harvested just melted my heart.

So now you've all these wonderful Endeavors tomatoes in your kitchen while waiting for your own tomatoes to pop up. What to do? What to do? I can eat a tomato like it is an apple. It is juicy and delicious. And just what else besides just biting into one? Well, here are some suggestions. Hope you all still remember my pico de gallo (tomato salsa) recipe. And make sure that you have a margarita in one hand while the other hand is dipping into the salsa with those crispy tortilla chips.

And here are my other suggestions with those wonderful tomatoes:

- Grill them. First, marinate them in any kind of salad dressing. My favorite is balsamic vinaigrette. Slice the tomato in thick slices and let it soak in the dressing for at least one-half hour. Add a pinch of kosher salt for extra flavor. Yes, grill them on high heat till they are a little charred, and then move them to an area with milder heat. Then sprinkle your favorite cheese on top. When the cheese melted, it's ready. Sprinkle some fresh chopped basil or tarragon or whatever you have in your garden on top, and no matter what you are serving, folks will go nuts!

• Salsa – yes, make pico de gallo. I don't want to take up the precious space here. Look it up on my Cinco de Mayo column.

Very simple but delicious recipe indeed – fresh tomatoes, onions, lime, celery, jalapenos and cilantro. Yes, life is good. Make sure that you've plenty of tortilla chips. And, of course, that the margaritas are cold!

• Marinated tomatoes. I am spoiled, marinating those lovely sliced tomatoes in different salad dressings is so easy and simple. And they last for at least a week or two. I've had great success with:

• Italian dressing
• Balsamic vinegar
• Blue cheese dressing
• Ranch dressing
• Thousand Island dressing

• Bloody Mary mix – with or without vodka. Just put a bunch of fresh tomatoes in your blender and add celery salt, Worcestershire sauce, Tabasco and a hint of Italian dressing. And you have your own Sunday concoction that everyone will go crazy over.

• Bruschetta – please pronounce it as "broos-ka-ta" and not "bros-shu-ta." I almost got my head bitten off one time by my colleague, who is a true Italian, when I told the class how much fun it is to make them. Actually it is very simple – serve the Italian pico de gallo over garlic toast.

There are hundreds and thousands of recipes of what we can do with those delicious tomatoes. I'm glad to discover Endeavors from Irene and Robin. What a great place! Hope you folks will enjoy them, too.

Portuguese chicken

A few weeks ago, some old friends that I grew up with came all the way from Toronto, Canada, to visit our humble abode here in the North Woods. That was such a joy! I love Toronto; it is such a modernized city, clean and fast-paced. I thought driving in Chicago or downtown Minneapolis was a venture, but driving in Toronto is a totally different trip. I am a turtle, always obeying the speed limit sign. How can these guys speed past me when I am already driving 75 mph? Oh, I forgot, they use kilometers instead. Does it mean that they can drive faster (ha ha)? And the police don't even seem to care.

Anyway, I love Toronto, not only because a lot of my bosom buddies live there, but also there are tons of great Chinese restaurants specializing in cuisines from all different regions: Cantonese, Szechuan, Hunan, Chiu Jau, Hakka, Peking, you name it. I was told that if you dine in a different restaurant every evening, it will take a few years to visit them all. What a dream indeed! And on top of that, there is an Oriental grocery store on almost every block. Totally amazing! There would be lobsters and live crabs squirming in the tanks and live carps and tilapias, eels and flounders, all waiting for their final fate. My wife is from the Midwest, and when I first took her shopping in the market, she thought it was an aquarium. Yes, it was an aquarium, indeed, but we eat the exhibits!

After showing my buddies all the favorite local tourist spots here, what was left to do? Well, first was to sample all the local breweries and then the craft beers from other areas. It took some time. And after a week, it is sad to say that we hadn't even covered our own 10-mile territory. So, instead of quoting MacArthur's favorite words, "I shall return," they unanimously said, "Oh, we have to come back soon."

So, besides the beer, I made them brats. Yes, brats (pronounced bra-ats) to the non-Wisconsinites, served, of course, with sauteed shredded onions slowly cooked with (what else but) our local beer. My buddies loved the whole routine. Too bad customs has a limit on packaged beer to bring across the border, or they would have loaded up their trunks with a smile.

While most of my old buddies were born in Hong Kong, quite a few came from different regions of China, migrating to Hong Kong when their parents escaped the communist regime during the '50s. One of my buddies is from Macao, a tiny peninsula not too far from Hong Kong. While Hong Kong was ceded to the British and became a British colony, Macao was "loaned" to the Portuguese and was ruled under their government. Looking back, that was totally absurd and ridiculous. Can you imagine a foreign country (say Japan) coming to the States, and claiming that they would take over Arizona for a hundred years? They would rule Arizona with its own government, with policies and legislatures with which America has no authority to question or interfere. Would we stand for that at all? Absolutely not, not even for a half second. But somehow, the Chinese would let foreign countries "do their thing" in their own country. I don't want to get into more details as that's not the purpose of this column. But, somehow, the story leads to the Portuguese chicken that my buddy made for us one evening.

I remember vacationing in Macao a few times while growing up. While gambling was banned in Hong Kong, they had casinos everywhere in Macao. It was "the Oriental Monte Carlo" then, and is still the Oriental Monte Carlo these days, putting Las Vegas to shame.

Anyway, while visiting Macao, there was a restaurant that I will always remember, as they featured two of my favorite dishes, Portuguese chicken and deep-fried squab. We all know what chicken is. But squab is another term for pigeon. Yes, pigeon. No, I don't think the chef would go under the road bridge to catch them, but I was told that they were farm raised. They were cleaned, deep-fried and served with a five-spice seasoning salt. The skin was delicate and crispy, and the meat was moist and flavorful.

So, my buddy who grew up in Macao volunteered to make my favorite dish. What can I say? Seagulls and crows are plentiful here, but pigeons? No. So, we'll stick with the

Portuguese chicken. It was an evening of fun, drinking and songs, eating and more songs, and more drinking and more songs. Oh, how I miss the good old days.

My buddy gave me his recipes while he was cooking. It was passed on to him by his godmother who was a chef for a loyal Portuguese family back in the '50s. Nothing was written down, but somehow we all remembered, after a few drinks. So, here is the true recipe that I'll share with you all:

Portuguese chicken
   1 whole quartered chicken, seasoned with salt and pepper
   4 cloves of minced garlic
   2 onions, quartered
   2 potatoes, quartered
   4 oz. package of baby carrots
   1 can coconut milk
   1 can condensed milk
   1 tablespoon curry powder
   1 teaspoon curry paste
   1 tablespoon chicken bouillon
   1 teaspoon brown sugar

In a large skillet, add a little oil and add garlic and onions. Brown chicken pieces till halfway done, then add potatoes and carrots. Brown for another two minutes, then add all the sauce mix. Let simmer for one-half hour to 45 minutes. Season to taste. Add more curry powder or sugar. When potatoes are tender, chicken should be just right.

The trick of this dish is to serve when the chicken is just tender and not overcooked. The sauce should be rich and thick. Thicken with cornstarch if necessary.

You folks should know how to make rice by now. Cook your rice and add shredded coconut with raisins into your rice. Mix well, and put the Portuguese chicken over the rice and serve. You'll be the hero, and bon appetit.

Spring roll or egg roll?

I have been teaching cooking classes all over the place. What a great way to make new friends. I teach community education classes at Spooner, River Falls, Amery and Balsam Lake. And each class has between eight to 18 students. Tentatively, I have made over 100-plus new friends over the year. And how do I remember all their names? Well, I cheated. I am known to be terrible with names, and on top of that, with no sense of direction. I would be lost even have my GPS on. It's pathetic. Oh well, unlike Mary Poppins, I can't be perfect in every which way.

Spring roll

It does bring a lot of joy in my teaching classes when students tell me how much they enjoy the classes:

• "How can it be so simple in making those dishes, and they are delicious."

• "Wait, you mean that's it? That's all it takes?"

• "What about those fancy gadgets I saw the chefs use on the food channels? I don't need them?"

• "My wife has a pantry filled with all kinds of sauces. Yet, these few are all I needed?"

• "I've never liked pot stickers, but these are delicious."

• "This is the best chow mein that I've ever tasted."

• "I made a dinner for my family who don't like Chinese food. And they loved it!"

Yes, cooking is a passion, you've got to love it. I have tried to simplify the cooking methods and with the ingredients, so you don't need to do a lot of prepping, nor need a lot of different special sauces or materials to make a delicious dish. One of the most popular appetizer is egg roll. And no one believes just how simple it is to make them.

Well, while most restaurants label them egg roll on their menu, actually they should be called spring roll instead. There is a product in the Orient called egg roll, and it is made with a semisweet egg batter. On a heated grill, the master would pour an ounce of batter on the grill and skillfully roll it to form a round biscuit roll with a single chopstick. In a minute, the master can roll over 100 of those egg rolls, and pack them neatly inside a gift box. It is flaky and crunchy, but oh, they are delicate and delicious.

Back to our egg roll. There are two kinds of wrappers – the regular egg roll wrappers, which are thick and doughy. But that's what they carry in most markets. Another one is called spring roll wrapper. Needless to say, that's what I would use. It is light, crispy and crunchy, as a spring roll should be. Usually, there are about 20-25 wrappers in each package, and you have to carefully peel them off one by one. So, what to stuff with? Aha, we can make the vegetarian version, or with any kind of meat that we desire – pork, beef, chicken or even venison. But the meat has to be sliced really thin, and cooked three-fourths through before we wrap them up.

Spring Roll
Ingredients (for 20 spring roll)
    1 package spring roll wrappers
    1 lb. shredded thin cabbage
    8 oz. shredded thin carrots
    4 oz. soaked and shredded wood ear (mushrooms)
    4 oz. bean sprouts
    8 oz. sliced thin meat, optional

Method:
    In a heated wok/nonstick pan, add 1 oz. oil, and add all vegetable mix. Add 1 tsp of chicken base, and 1 T of oyster sauce. Cook till three-fourths done. And set aside.
    On a clean cutting board, put one piece of wrapper diagonally on board, brush the top edges with egg wash (an egg beaten with a little water). Place 2 oz. of the vegetable

mix at the bottom, and carefully roll the wrapper up. Fold the wrapper ends toward center and keep rolling till it forms a perfect roll. Set them on a flat tray dusted with cornstarch (so it won't stick).

You can actually have a spring roll party and roll tons of these and freeze them for later use. Make sure you flash freeze them in the freezer first, ina single layer, and store them in a zipper bag – 15 to 20 in each bag. The frozen ones should last six to nine months in the freezer. And they are just as delicious.

You can add your favorite meat to the spring roll, but I usually just make them vegetarian style. And to cook them, very easy and simple.

Procedure:

Heat up wok/frying pan with 1 inch of oil. Place spring roll six to eight at a time in heated oil. Flip each to the other side when one side is brown. On a separate plate, place some paper towels to absorb extra grease, and place spring rolls on top. And ready to serve when all spring rolls are done.

But, not yet! We'll need our dipping sauce. While most Chinese restaurants would create their own sweet-and-sour dipping sauce, made with sugar, vinegar and No. 2 red dye, I've created a healthy and simple sauce. Ready?

1 jar (8 to 12 oz.) orange marmalade
1 can (8 to 12 oz.) crushed pineapple

Mix the two together, and there is our dipping sauce. Enjoy!

The spring roll wrappers are carried in Oriental grocery stores only. So, use the regular egg roll wrapper if you have to. It is the fun and getting together that counts. And for those daring and adventurous, add 1 T of chili paste to your dipping sauce. And watch your guests go "oooh" or "ahhhh." Yes, simple pleasure in life that is rather inexpensive.

So, let's talk about wine pairing. Actually, spring rolls go well with just about any kind of beer. But of course, with dark beer is my favorite. And with wine, what shall we choose?

We talked about the Yin and Yan earlier, the balance of soft and smooth versus the strong tasting. Well, think about it, the spring rolls are crispy and crunchy, while the sauce is sweet and pungent. Just how to balance the flavors? There are two wines that come in mind – Pinot Grigio, or gewurtztraminer. Pinot Gris/Grigio is a semi-dry, white wine, and Gewurtz is a semisweet wine but with a bite to it. Both wines are great complements to the spring roll. So, enjoy them.

Eating is an experience.

Keep on rock and rolling

I am most grateful for all the positive comments that we have received so far. Thank you so very much for your kind support. Can't believe another year just flew by. Somehow, I feel that 2016 is going to be a great year for all of us – eat well, stay healthy and active, and maintain that positive attitude; good things will keep happening.

Our menu was missing Hawaiian (sweet and sour) chicken last week because of limited column space. So, we will make up for it today, with crab Rangoon as the additional appetizer. How's that?

So now, practice on our first menu till you are absolutely pleased and comfortable with each item, and you'll be well on your way to becoming an expert. Don't forget, the recipe here is just a guideline, use your imagination and adjust it any way you like (or your guests would like) – more sugar if you want it sweeter, or add vinegar if you like it "puckerier."

Our first Wok & Roll menu:
Pot stickers (Wor Teh) with dipping sauce
Crab Rangoon
Beef & broccoli Cantonese
Hawaiian (sweet and sour) chicken
Steamed jasmine rice
We already went over the pot stickers, beef and broccoli and steamed jasmine rice. So, let's focus on the crab Rangoon and the Hawaiian chicken.

Crab Rangoon:
Ingredients: wrappers (same as the pot stickers, but get the square kind), cream cheese, 6 oz.; sea legs (imitation crabmeat) 4 oz.; and egg wash.

Methods: Dust your counter first, to make sure that the wrappers don't stick to each other. In a bowl, add cream cheese and sea legs, mix well. Lay six to eight wrappers on counter, and add 1 tsp. of sea legs mix to each wrapper. Brush half of the edge, and fold the other half over. Crimp the corners together, and there you have it. Line them up in a flat pan dusted with flour or cornstarch for later use.

Hawaiian chicken (for 4):
Ingredients:
1 lb. chicken, boneless thigh; cornstarch/flour; egg wash; panko (Japanese bread crumbs).
Sauces:
Crushed pineapple (small can), marmalade, vinegar, sugar, wine and ketchup (optional).
Methods:
Cut chicken into bite size (2" x 1/2") and season with salt and pepper. Dust chicken generously with flour/ cornstarch mix; put chicken in egg wash, and then coat with panko (or regular bread crumbs). Set aside.

Sauces: Heat up 2 cups of wine, and add 1/2 can crushed pineapple; add 1/2 cup marmalade. Mix well. Add 1/4 cup of vinegar and 1/4 cup of sugar to taste (adjust to your liking). Thicken with cornstarch mix if it is too thin and runny. You can use the sauce as dipping sauce for both the crab Rangoon and the Hawaiian chicken.

Heat up your frying pan, and add 2" of oil. When oil is hot (sprinkle a drop of wine into oil, it splashes), then add crab Rangoon to oil, six to eight at a time. Take them out with strainer and put on a plate with paper towel to absorb the grease. Put them on a decorative plate with a bowl for sauce. Enjoy!

After crab Rangoon, cook the chicken and brown both sides. When cooked, two to three minutes, strain them out and put on a piece of paper towel. Put on a decorative plate, and pour sauces on top, or mix them in a large bowl and then put on the platter. Garnish the plate with halved pineapple rings around (with a halved cherry on each piece), and you'll be the hero!

Enjoy your festive New Year's dinner! I would recommend something dry and spicy as the Hawaiian dish is a bit sweet. Try sauvignon blanc or gewurztraminer. Enjoy!

Popular dim sum - Siu Mai

Have some dim sum fun

Most people have never heard of dim sum, not to
mention actually trying them. Growing up in Hong
Kong, dim sum is popular like the Big Mac, except that there
is no Happy Meal version. In straight translation, dim means
touch and sum is your heart. So, a touch of your heart. Can
you visualize that a certain food can actually touch your
heart? Well, it sure did to me for many, many years. It was,
and still is, a tradition on
weekends and holidays;
folks will gather with their
families and friends in
dim sum houses to have
some comfort foods and
to chat and catch up. It
is amazing that at every
dim sum house, there
will be a long line waiting
even though the house is
already packed. You take
a number, and then you
just patiently wait till your
number is called. Most

*Dim sum - char siu bao
Steamed buns stuffed with
barbecued pork*

restaurants won't even bother with taking reservations, it's all first come, first serve.

So, what's the magic about dim sum houses that makes them so intriguing? Let me explain the ritual from the very beginning. Dim sums are tasty bite-size morsels that are made with shrimp, pork, beef, tofu and whatever the chefs created. They can be steamed, baked, fried, braised, stuffed or sauteed. And there are at least a hundred, if not more, varieties. They are served either in a bamboo steamer or on small plates, like the tapas. The tradition began hundreds of years ago. It is a place to socialize, to do business, and to get some relaxation and great foods. It has become a daily routine called "yum cha," drink tea. And here is the ritual:

After your number is called, and you get seated, first thing the server asks will be, "What kind of tea would you prefer?" Most teahouses are stocked with high-quality teas, and they do charge you accordingly. Most of them charge $1 to $2 per person. So, know your tea, and don't get tea bags! There are red teas and green teas. Red teas include oolong, pu-erh, Dragon Well and lychee red. These teas are stronger and rich with flavors. And then there are the green teas. Most popular are jasmine flower and chrysanthemum, and a new combination called "goak poh," which is a combination of pu-erh and chrysanthemum. Anyway, do not pour the tea right away, let it brew three to five minutes. That's the fun of yum cha, you take your time in enjoying everything. No more eat and run, or eat while you run. Now is the time to enjoy every moment.

Soon you will notice cart after cart of foods passing you by. Those carts are equipped with steamers at the bottom, so whatever foods they are carrying are guaranteed to be piping hot when they reach your table. However, those carts will not stop at your table unless you wave them down. So, you have to start learning what you would like to order. Actually, most of the dishes are very popular in the U.S., except these few:

• **Chicken feet** – you have to develop a taste for it. It is the same watching someone munching on pork's feet the first time.

• **Beef tripe** – once you try them, you'll love them, but …

- **Baby octopus** – especially in curry sauce. But it is hard to eat anything with tentacles still attached.

So, here are my 10 favorites, you can't go wrong with them. And even if it's your first time, just ask your server to get them for you, they'll be most happy to oblige:

- **Har gow** – rice wrapper stuffed with shrimp and bamboo shoots. Steamed.
- **Siu mai** – dumpling filled with minced pork and shiitake mushroom. Steamed.
- **Spring roll** – light and crispy. One is filled with shredded
   vegetables and the other with shrimp. Deep-fried.
- **Char siu bao** – buns stuffed with tasty barbecued pork. Steamed or baked.
- **Nin yung bao** – buns stuffed with mashed sweet lotus seed. Steamed.
- **Wu kok** – taro roots mixed with seasoned pork, dipped in a batter then deep-fried.
- **Cheung Fun** – steamed rice noodles filled with either shrimp, beef or barbecued pork. The sweet soya sauce to pour over enhances the flavors.
- **Lo bak go** – made with daikon radish. Comes lightly pan fried. A lot of work goes in the making. Your first bite will tell you.
- **Pot stickers** – stuffed with minced pork and dipped in a ginger soya sauce.
- All depends on the chef, I have experienced many dishes that I have never heard of – stuffed eggplant with minced seafood mix, shrimp wrapped with seaweed ... so be adventurous.

While you enjoy the food and conversations, observe these few simple rules:

- When your teapot is empty, just move the lid to the side. No need to try to get your server's attention. I'll explain why later.
- When someone pours tea for you, respond with tapping the table with your second and third fingers. They represent your head, and you're bowing back to say thanks.

And oh, one more thing – your table receives a ticket

FOOD

Chinese deli

when you're seated. The ticket has different prices of each dish. The server will circle the dish when it is delivered to you. When you're done eating, they simply add up the different numbers of dishes you ordered and then you just pay the cashier. Easy and simple.

Now you have it, enjoy. The sad thing is that there are not too many dim sum houses here in Wisconsin, so we have to travel west to Minnesota. But the trip is well worth it.

Rice noodles "cheun fun"

62

A royal Danish treat

I've lived in many different places in the U.S. – Southern California, Texas, Georgia and finally, Wisconsin; from the Deep South to the "deep North." What an experience indeed! Especially sinceI was born in Hong Kong, a land with a totally different culture and lifestyles. With 98 percent of the population being Chinese, it was easy to blend in when you are Chinese. In California, it was still easy living, as folks were used to the early immigrants from China. They were just about everywhere! Living in Texas was a bit different, I still remember the shock when my son came home from school one day and said, "Hi y'all" to us when he walked in the door. However, living in Georgia was a little tense, as the Southerners have never forgotten that they lost the war. They still remember in detail how Atlanta was burnt to the ground. Then, living in Milwaukee was a treat after all. A land of beauty with early immigrants from all over – Germany, Italy, Poland and many other European countries. Somehow, I managed to blend in, and life was good. However, moving to the North Woods, life is even better.

Most of the folks I meet are from here. I mean, they were born here and have spent their whole lives working and living here and nowhere else. A bit different than when we were living in Atlanta – when everyone we met was from someplace else. I remember our old neighborhood - the cul-de-sac that housed 20-some families, yet there were only two families that were actually born in Atlanta. Others were from various states, moved into the area just to work for the big corporations that have their headquarters stationed in Atlanta – Coca-Cola, IBM, UPS, Arby's, Home Depot and hundreds of financial institutions.

I never met any Swedish friends till we moved up here two years ago. Holy smoke, all of a sudden, they are everywhere. Have to be honest, I knew nothing about the Danish and Swedish cuisines; yet slowly and surely, I learn a bit more here and there, and I am in awe. First, I heard about this "lutefisk." Don't think I will go that far even though I am in the food business. Then my good friend, Roger Nielsen and his lovely wife, Vicki, invited us to their home in Sarona for a Danish feast. I was in for a surprise, as I have never encountered Dan- ish food in my life.

Roger and Vicki took the cooking classes that I offered through the Spooner Community Education. We've become good friends, as they have become my "groupies" – attending my barbershop concert in Amery, all my cooking classes at Spooner, and even the special event (the Chinese dinner at Spooner Golf Course) in Spooner. Anyway, I'd no clue what to expect when they invited my wife and I to his Danish feast.

And lo and behold, that was some feast, indeed! I'll take the pleasure to walk you through. Read this with a smile and have a napkin close by. We started out with an Aquavit Bloody Mary to whet the appetite. I've never tasted aquavit before, it tastes like vodka, but with a different kick. Like vodka, it can be made with different ingredients (besides potatoes) and are imported from different countries – Denmark, Norway, Sweden and U.S. That was treat No. 1, the beginning of a seven-course meal.

The courses continued, with open-faced sandwiches with different ingredients – different styles of pickled herrings, liver pate, pork sausages and assorted cheese. All with a toast of different aquavit in between. Roger instructed us to say "skal" (sounds like "skol") before the toasting. No clinking of the glass, but yet, look the guests in the eyes and then empty the glass. That was treat No. 3 (and many more lost count after nine), a toast from the heart through the meeting of the eyes. I like that very much.

A small wood plank was set next to the table setting, and three or four kinds of bread were set in the basket – rye, Vienna bread and some dark bread, and all were delicious.

We were told that the bread must be generously and evenly spread with butter from one end to the other before consum- ing. The Carlsberg beers kept floating around. I had Carlsberg beer a long time ago in Hong Kong, a match of San Miguel, a local brew. Still tasted same after all these years, but much bet- ter with each course. Then came the different herrings – plain, with mustard and wine sauce. They all tasted wonderful, with or without the Carlsberg beer; and that was just the beginning. The sausage platter, the egg salad with shrimp rolled along; I was full before the cheese platter hit the table (a combination of Russian Havarti, Tilsit and Danish Blue, garnished with peppers, radish and grapes). I had another bite even though my body said "No more, please." But it was worth it. Then came the dessert; my brain stopped talking to me when I went for just "a little tiny bite."

Conversations flowed with the ongoing aquavit between each course, different flavors from different countries – Denmark, Norway, Sweden and even U.S. I've never tasted aquavit before, and that was an experience in itself. I have learnt to say 'Bottoms up.' 'Salud,' 'Gan bei' and 'Salute' with different friends, but 'Skal' has a new meaning – look into your friends' eyes and drink up. The meeting of the minds and souls indeed. I love that.

The china set that the food was served on is another story. I noticed a hint of the Oriental flair on the pattern of the set, just to find out that back in the 1700s, the king of Denmark did visit China, and upon his return to his homeland, he brought one of the best porcelain makers with him; and hence, the best Danish porcelain with a Chinese touch was created. I was touched. Kept me wondering why the pickled herring has no soya sauce in it!

Thanks to Roger and Vicki for the most memorable Danish meal. "Skal."

The best fried rice

Without a doubt, fried rice is my very favorite comfort food. It is easy to make, tasty and inexpensive (the magic word; my budget for food and beverage during college days was $5 a week. Guess how much was for food and how much was for "beverage.") However, I ate well and stayed healthy, thank goodness for my PaoPao's (grandma's) fried rice recipe.

To have the best fried rice, we have to start with a perfect batch of cooked rice. A lot of folks ask me just how to cook rice. Being Chinese, I shiver looking at boxes of Uncle Ben's "parboiled" rice in the market. Just what is parboiled rice? I've never tried it and have no intention to (sorry, Uncle Ben). I got my secret recipe from my PaoPao, and I am going to share that with you all here. Follow these simple steps. I never use any measuring cups but, somehow, the rice comes out perfect each and every time. If you are not the adventurous type, invest $20 and get an electric rice cooker.

So, here it goes:
• Pick the right size pot with tight-fitting lid.
• Put one handful of rice for each guest in the pot. If you have four people eating, put in four handfuls of rice. Always add one more handful for the house, just in case someone has a bigger appetite.
• Rinse the rice with cold running water to wash out the dust and dirt.
• Put the pot on the stove, add water. How much water? Well, here is the trick – take your second finger, let the tip just touch the rice, and add water so the water level reaches the first joint. That's all the water you will need. Pretty scientific, eh? Oh, if you would like your rice to glisten and shine, add one-fourth cup of oil to the water.
• Heat up the stove and bring water to a boil. When the water starts bubbling, turn heat down to simmer. Cover with lid. Set it and forget it.
• The rice is usually cooked after 15 to 20 minutes, but simmering on low heat is fine for at least one-half hour or more.

FOOD

So, you have perfect steamed rice, now what? Every time I make rice, I cook more than I need and use the leftovers for fried rice later. Leave the leftover rice in the refrigerator overnight for best results. Now, ready for the best fried rice ever?

Get all the ingredients you need first, and set them on the counter. The worst part of cooking is when you have to scrounge for products that you need right in the middle of cooking. So here is the list (or mise en place, remember?)

- A nonstick wok, two spatulas, oil, salt and pepper, eggs, frozen peas and carrots, and your choice of meats.
- Take the rice out from the refrigerator and break it down by rubbing them gently so they won't stick together.
- Heat up the wok, scramble the eggs. Add a tablespoon of oil in heated wok and pour egg batter in. Use the spatula to break the eggs in smaller pieces and set aside.
- Heat up wok again, then add rice. Gently stir rice around, making sure that they don't stick to the wok. Add a little oil if you prefer, but it is not necessary with a nonstick wok.
- While the rice is getting heated up, add salt and pepper to taste.
- While most restaurant use soya sauce for color and flavor, I prefer oyster sauce. I like the distinctive taste and that it adds a darker color to the rice.
- Keep turning the rice with your spatulas and adjust the seasoning to taste. When the rice is hot to touch, add frozen peas, carrots and choice of precooked meat. I personally love to put whatever leftovers I have from the night before, just make sure that they are diced up in smaller pieces.
- Add the cooked eggs right before serving and sprinkle with shredded scallions on top for extra color and flavors.

There you have it. My favorite meats are the tasty leftovers, such as diced ham, turkey, pork chops, etc. Nothing goes to waste. You can also make a combo fried rice with shrimp, barbecue pork, eggs and whatever else you like. We have a fancy name for that, "yang chow fried rice." You can serve that by itself or in banquet style, with Hawaiian chicken and Szechuan beef. And bless your foods with a glass of Gewurztraminer. Oh, life is good, enjoy!

General Tso's Chicken

A lot of Chinese restaurants in the States serve General Tso's Chicken. But just like Chop Suey and Fortune Cookies, they are totally unknown to the native Chinese. Unlike Colonel Sanders who created his famous "Finger licking Chicken with 10 secret herbs and spices", there is no living proof that General Tso has anything to do with this famous dish. And we don't even know that if General Tso even liked the taste of chicken. So, where is the connection?

That's something charming and romantic about food and beverage, many memorable entrees or drinks were created a long time ago, and somehow remain famous after many generations. Do you know who created Caesar Salad? No, not Julius Caesar from the mighty Roman Empire, but by a chef named Caesar Cardini, who was an immigrant from Italy. It was in his restaurant in Tijuana, Mexico that he first introduced this famous salad.

And how about Margaritas? They are found in Block Letters in most menus of Mexican Restaurants, but who created it? And funny, both versions involved Tijuana, Mexico. Tijuana must have been a swinging town then. Well, one version is that in 1938, a restaurateur named Carlos "Danny" Herrera who wanted to please the famous movie star Majorie King, but she couldn't drink the popular tequila because it was too potent. So, he blended some sweetened lime juice with Triple Sec (an orange flavored liqueur) and mixed them with tequila and then served her. And she loved it.

Another story surfaced 10 years later. A Dallas socialite named Margarita Sames served a special drink for her party hosted at her home in Acapulco, Mexico. (Yes, still involved Mexico). Her guests loved the drink. And one of the guests was Tommy Hilton, the owner of the famous hotel chain. He brought the recipe back to the States and introduced it to his hotels. And the name 'Margarita' became a household word overnight.

Yes, General Tso did exist, but there was no proof that he created the famous dish. He was indeed a general in the Qing Dynasty. Actually, his name is pronounced as Juo (not Tso) Jung Tang. He led his army and defeated the Taiping

Rebellion (1862 – 1877). He was considered a hero in his hometown of Hunan, which is famous for its spicy cooking. However, one cannot find "General Tso's Chicken" served in any restaurants in Hunan, or even in China. So, who should take the credit?

Though many chefs have claimed ownership through all these years, this one story has the most credibility. There was a chef named Peng Chang Kwei (or P.C. Kwei) who was one of the master chefs for General Cheng Kai Shek. Then, when the communists took over China after WWII, the National Party fled to the little island of Taiwan. During the 60's, Kwei and his family migrated to the States and settled down in New York City. Kwei eventually opened a restaurant. He specialized in Hunan cooking, which is hot and spicy, and the American folks weren't very keen of spicy foods then. So, seeing that Sweet and Sour Pork was very popular with the Americans, chef Kwei took one of his favorite chicken dishes, and modified it with a sweet and spicy sauce. He didn't have a name for the new creation yet. Then, he remembered his childhood hero General Tso Jung Tang, and named the dish after him. Hence, General Tso's Chicken was born! It was an instant success. Even Henry Kissinger favored the dish, and had a picture taken with chef Kwei which still hangs in the restaurant!

There are hundred versions of how to make General Tso's Chicken, and they are all tasty and yummy. But, wouldn't it be funny if General Tso was still alive, just to see his name connected to chicken, if he was a vegetarian?

So, let's get serious and cook us some great food. I modified the recipe somewhat and come up with my own version. I tested it on my friends and neighbors, and they all give me the thumbs up.

GENERAL TSO'S CHICKEN: (feeds 4)
Ingredients:

Chicken cubed	1 lb. (I personally like dark meat)
Egg whites	3 ea.
Corn Starch	½ Cup
Flour	½ Cup
Chili Pods	7 – 10 ea.
Salt & Pepper to taste	

Sauce:

Chili Paste	1 tsp. *(add more if you like hot and spicy)*
Corn Starch	8 tsp
White Wine	2 Cups
Vinegar	¼ Cup
Brown Sugar	2 TB
Soya Sauce	2 TB
Plum Sauce	4 TB (same as Hoi Sin Sauce)
Ketchup	2 TB
Marmalade	2 TB

Method:

Pat dry chicken pieces, season to taste, and dip in egg white, then corn starch & flour mix (most recipes just call for corn starch, but the added flour will give the chicken a softer crunch, and more golden brown). Heat up wok/pan and add 2" oil. Brown all pieces, 6 – 8 pieces at a time (center of chicken should be white, not pink). Pick up and place on plate with paper towels to absorb excess grease. In separate pot, add 2 TB oil, and add chili pods, then add all sauce ingredients and gently stir till it thickens (if it is too thick, add more water/wine). Taste the sauce to your liking – add more sugar if you like more sweet, or add vinegar if you like more 'puck'.

Add fried chicken to the sauce, make sure that all pieces are nicely coated. Serve with steamed Jasmine rice. And for garnish, circle the plate with steamed broccoli crowns (that's optional).

Enjoy! And may the spirit of General Tso be with you.

FOOD

Coconut shrimp

My goodness, it has been a year since we moved up here to the North Woods. My wife and I knew nothing about the area, except all the horror stories our friends warned us about, like getting buried in 10 to 15 feet of snow in the winter or that deer are running wild on the highways. Well, I haven't hit a deer yet (knock on wood), but I did have a 50-pound wild turkey hit and smash my windshield. Scared the daylight out of me, as I didn't even see it coming. I think that, after $2,500 of damage, that qualifies me to be an unofficial country boy.

It has been an amazing journey indeed. After we decided to move out of Milwaukee to be closer to our granddaughter who resides in the Twin Cities, we sold our house, bought a new home, moved and settled in, all within 60 days. Yes, and my amazing wife did all the work while I was complaining about the headache of moving. Needless to say, I have to pamper her, that's the least I can do. "We've got to celebrate our new life here," I said. "What can I make you for dinner?"

I used to ask her that every time I went shopping but, somehow, I never make the dinner that she asked for. When I go shopping, I always search for what looks fresh and what's on sale. So, yes, I knew what I wanted to make, but if I saw something nice and fresh in the market, or something with a good price, I would buy those things first and then figure out what to do with them when I got home. This time she had that serious look in her face and I dare not alter her wish. After all, I like sleeping in my bed. She said, "I'd like coconut shrimp for our special dinner." So, coconut shrimp it was, to celebrate our first anniversary at our new home.

Most chain restaurants offer coconut shrimp as either an appetizer or as an entree. Either way, they are cooked from a frozen package. Sure, they're still quite tasty, but not the same as the ones you make from scratch. It is really simple, but you have to follow each step carefully to make it right.

Coconut shrimp with marmalade dipping sauce, for four
Ingredients:
- 1 lb. large raw shrimp, peeled and deveined
- 1/2 cup flour
- 1/2 cup cornstarch
- 1/8 tsp. each salt and pepper
- 4 eggs, beaten
- 2 cups sweetened shredded coconut

Sauce:
- 1 cup marmalade
- 1 can (6-8 oz.) crushed pineapple

There are different sizes of shrimp, ranked 12-16 (large), 16-25 (medium), 25-30 (small), etc. All the ranking is, is the sizes - the smaller the number, the larger the shrimp. They are measured by how many shrimp there are in a pound. Also, look for the "P&D," means peeled and deveined, it might cost a little bit more but it saves you the hazard of trying to peel them and to get those little tiny veins out from the back of the shrimp.

Shrimp can come from Vietnam, Thailand, China, India and the Gulf Coast, with different flavor depending on what they feed on. Regardless, once you pick out the vein (which is sandy), most shrimp are tasty.

Method:
- Thaw and rinse the shrimp, and then butterfly them. Butterfly cut is to cut them slightly in the middle and unfold them to look like a donut.
- Bread them lightly with the seasoned cornstarch and flour mix. I like this mix because cornstarch gives the crispiness and flour gives the color.
- Dip them in the egg batter.
- Press them in the coconut flakes.

I would recommend use the left hand for dipping and the right hand for breading, otherwise your fingers will be cemented with saute coconut batter.

In a heated saute pan, add 2" of oil. Fry the breaded shrimp over medium heat on one side, flip and do same with the

FOOD

other side. When golden brown, set aside on a platter with a paper towel to absorb the extra grease.

Make the marmalade and pineapple salsa with half of each and mix well, e.g. 4 oz. of marmalade with 4 oz. of pineapple tidbits. Add 1/2 to 1 tsp. of chile paste for guests who like hot and spicy. Set the golden coconut shrimp on a platter with shredded lettuce at the bottom. Garnish with pineapple chunks on edge around the plate. You'll be the hero.

You may have leftover egg batter and shredded coconut. Heat up saute pan, and add 1 tbs. of oil. Fry the egg and coconut batter first, then add to steamed rice with some raisins. Mix well, add salt and pepper to taste.

We talked about the Endeavors tomatoes last week. If you can get your hands on some, cut some thick slices and sprinkle with grated Romano or Parmesan cheese on top with some finely chopped fresh garden herbs (I recommend tarragon or basil). Add a few drops of bleu cheese dressing on top and you'll have a perfect feast. I talked about the yin and yang of cooking, the balance of flavor, color and aroma. Normally, I would just add balsamic vinegar to the tomatoes, but it will clash with the flavor of the sweet and sour marmalade salsa.

If you have guests who are allergic to coconut, you can coat the shrimp with panko. The panko mix adds extra crispiness, and I find it is also good to bread chicken strips, pork strips and even vegetable strips for a good tempura side dish.

The pineapple and marmalade salsa is just an idea, you can use whatever your imagination will carry. Try it with raspberries, strawberries or any melons that you can find.

Anyway, I know my wife will be pleased. I hope your coconut shrimp will be a success also.

Sauces from different regions

We talked about the foods from different regions last week. So, do you feel better now knowing that the Cantonese cuisine from the South is very different from the Peking entrees from the North? Not only the cooking methods are different, but also the ingredients; mainly, the sauces the chefs choose for their regional dishes.

The reason why foods from different regions are different is because of the ingredients available. (And that applies not only to Chinese foods – Mexican, Italian, French, German … all share the same philosophy, i.e., make do with what you got.) It is impossible to fully stock our kitchen with all kinds of different sauces. Our cupboards are not big enough to start with; and moreover, what is available in the market, how does each sauce taste? And how do we cook with them? Even though I grew up in Hong Kong and speak and write Chinese, there are so many sauces in the Oriental grocery store that I have never heard of, nor have ever used before; even I have problems knowing which one to choose.

So, let me just give a brief description of my own inventory, something that I need to have for my Chinese cooking:

Soy sauce – a must-have in the kitchen, for dipping, marinades or just cooking. It is made from fermented soybeans. And Kikkoman is actually made here in Wisconsin!

Oyster sauce – a thick, pungent sauce made from oyster extract. But these days, it is mostly made with artificial flavors.

Black bean sauce w/minced garlic - It is made with fermented black beans, mixed with minced garlic. By itself it smells terrible, but when added to the food, it is heavenly. I never cook without it.

Hoisin sauce (or plum sauce) - A must with Mu Shu's, Peking Duck and lotus blossoms. It is dark, sweet and pungent. That and hot mustard are great dipping sauce companions for any appetizers. (Forget the duck sauce. Don't even know where it comes from. And trust me, there are no parts of any ducks involved in the manufacturing process.)

Roasted sesame oil -Another all-time favorite. Very aromatic, and adds a glisten to your foods.

Fish sauce - A product from Thailand or Vietnam. Adds a unique flavor to your food. Made with fermented fish. Those who love lutefisk will find this sauce totally irresistible.

Five spice powder – Made with star anise, fennel seed, Szechuan pepper, cinnamon and cloves. Can you just feel the aromatic sensations? Great with stews or marinades.

Cooking wine – It adds a "zing" to the marinade and sauces. I use chardonnay or gewurztraminer, it's more convenient (for marinating and drinking).

My favorite line from W.C. Fields, "I love cooking with wine. Sometimes I even put it in the food."

Chili paste - My favorite is Lan Chee but there are newer brands from China, with a lot of good stuff at the bottom, and floats with a rich layer of spicy red chili oil. My newest thrill is Srirachai sauce. It is originated from Vietnam, made with fresh chili, vinegar and spices.

Garlic, scallions and ginger - I would hang the string of garlic by the window, and wrap the ginger with a paper towel and keep it next to the bunch of scallions in the refrigerator.

There are many other sauces made with fermented beans which I have yet to try. But, keep it simple. Try out a few ingredients that you are fond of and become comfortable with first, then broaden your horizon later.

Have fun and happy cooking.

Summer Concoctions

Summer is finally here. What a way to spend a hot muggy day – on your swinging hammock sipping on a nice chilled concoction. Yes, I know that living in Wisconsin, beers are our daily bread. But, let's spcan start with one liquor at a time, and eventually build up our own stock for all occasions. The most popular liquors are vodka, rum, gin, tequila and triple sec. And of course, we need juices from pineapples, oranges, limes and coconuts. So, are you ready to "wok & roll" with your blender?

I know that most folks drink their beers out of the can or bottle. So, let's get a little sophisticated and learn to drink beer out of a mug. The reason is that rather than spending a fortune on expensive glassware, like hurricane, margarita, tulip, highball or zombie, we just use a beer mug for all cocktails. Oh, the joy of living in Wisconsin. Now, what to do to set up your bar? Yes, the days of just using the bottle opener (or your teeth) are gone. First, we need a set of beer mugs – the size of the set depends on how many friends you have. Then, we need an electric blender, a mixing cup, either glass or metal, with a bar spoon, a 1-ounce shot glass and a cutting board with a paring knife (to cut cost, a pocket knife can do the same job). When you get more serious about making cocktails, then you can invest on getting picks, straws, swizzle sticks and napkins (with Packers logo, of course).

Oh, did I forget stocking your bar with brandy? Don't know why, but brandy is the most popular liquor in Wisconsin (outsold vodka and whisky). I've heard that there is a supper club in Sheboygan that serves a brandy manhattan in a tumbler for $4. There's always a wait for a table, and folks will have two to three brandy manhattans while waiting for their tables. No one has ever complained about the food. After two to three doubles, everything would taste great, don't you think? What a great strategy!

So, now that you are all set, what to do with your inventory? The first one is:

Long Island Iced Tea

Full your mug with ice, and then add:

1/2 oz. vodka
1/2 oz. gin
1/2 oz. tequila
1/2 oz. rum
1/2 oz. triple sec
2 oz. sweetened lime juice
Splash of Coke

Garnish with lemon twist. This is a most wicked drink (with 2.5 oz. of alcohol)! It tastes just like an ordinary iced tea. But it will give you a buzz in no time flat. And the hammock seems to be swinging on its own.

Margarita

1 oz. tequila
1/2 oz. triple sec
4 oz. sweetened lime juice

Blend the ingredients with ice. Garnish with lime wheel. I like to coat the rim of the mug with margarita salt, but that's optional. I would recommend just use the ordinary brand of tequila rather than using the named brands (Patron, Cuervo, etc.). It is cheaper, plus, after mixing up with lime juice, you can't tell the difference anyway. By the way, do you know that tequilas are made with the juice of the blue agave plant? All tequilas that are sold in the U.S. are produced in the area around the city of Tequila, in the state of Jalisco. Any tequilas that are produced outside of Jalisco are labeled mezcal.

And there are three categories of tequilas: silver, gold and anejo. Silver are the fresh distilled ones bottled directly from the distillery. And the gold has been aged in the white oak barrels imported from the States for at least a year or two. The anejo has been aged from two to four years in those barrels. Hence, a lot smoother, and are pricier.

Now that strawberries are in season, add some strawberries

in the blender and you've a strawberry margarita. And do same with mango, or whatever fruits that tickle your fancy.

Daiquiri

1 oz. rum
4 oz. sweetened lime juice
Blend well with ice. Use your imagination, throw in strawberries, and you've a strawberry daiquiri. Throw in a banana, and you got yourself a banana daiquiri. The list can go on and on.

Mai tai

1 oz. rum
1/2 oz. crème de almond
2 oz. sweetened lime juice
Blend well with ice and float with dark rum (Meyers).
Garnish with a cherry and a sprig of fresh mint from your garden.

I love rum. It is made from sugar cane, grown along the Caribbean belt – Puerto Rico, Cuba, Jamaica, the Virgin Islands, and of course, Hawaii. I heard a story that the old British navy promised a pint of rum each day for each sailor who signed up for an overseas excursion. Hmmm, a pint each day, not a bad idea.

Chi Chi

1 oz. vodka
1 oz. (Coco Lopez) cream of coconut
2 oz. pineapple juice
Blend well with ice and serve with a pineapple stalk.

While gin is made with juniper berries, and has a distinctive aroma and flavor; vodka has no aroma or taste at all. And yet, it is the most popular alcohol sold in the States. The old saying that vodka is made with potato remains an old saying. These days, vodka is made with grains. It is distilled at high proof to remove all congeners.

I consider myself a pretty good bartender, as I tried hard to learn about different brands of liquor and the thousands of recipes. But these days, I don't even recognize half of the recipes. And some are even obscene and vulgar.

Now, in closing, here is one of my all-time favorites, the zombie:

Zombie

1 oz. dark rum
1 oz. light rum
1/2 oz. crème de almond
1/2 oz. triple sec
1 oz. orange juice
1 oz. sweetened lime juice

Blend well with ice and top with 1/2 oz. 151 proof rum with cherry garnish. And swing really slow on your hammock. And have yourself a great summer!

Wine tasting 101

I knew nothing about wines when I first attended college. Beer, yes; wine, nada. It wasn't till I got a job working as a waiter in a steakhouse that I have to learn about different wines and wine and food pairing. I couldn't even pronounce the names, not to mention making recommendations to my customers. Try to pronounce Chateauneuf du Pape without spitting all over someone's face. So, I took the wine menu home, and actually studied it. I learned how to pronounce and describe the wines after many sleepless nights practicing. "Yes sir, this particular cabernet sauvignon has flavors of black cherry and dark berry, with a hint of toasted oak; and it should complement nicely with your filet mignon." I was a working student, and couldn't afford to pay $30 to $50 for a bottle of those expensive wine just for "education purposes." Lucky enough, the restaurant saved all the empty wine bottles (well, almost empty) so they could do an inventory every evening. And since the bartender and I were good friends, he would let me sit at the corner of the bar after my shift and taste whatever was left in the bottle. I would write down on my notepad the name of the wine, the year it was made, the name of the vintner, and the country of origin. And most important, how my palate felt about that particular wine. And that, my dear friends, was the beginning of my journey of wine tasting.

There are many wines in the market – mostly red, white and pink. As the name implies, red wines are made from red grapes and white wines from white grapes. And pink is a mix of both red and white grapes (as in white zinfandel). Wine is really a gift from the gods. We just pick the grapes off the vine, crush them and set them in a barrel. The yeast and the bacteria which live on the skin of the grapes will start to ferment. And slowly, it will turn the sugar in the grapes into alcohol and carbon dioxide. Of course, there is a lot more to the whole process, but in a nutshell, that's how grapes turn to wine, through natural fermentation.

If you know nothing about wine, looking at a wine menu in

a restaurant is most intimidating.

Trying to figure out what wine will pair with your dinner becomes a scientific experiment.

No worries. Follow these simple instructions and you can become a wine expert in no time flat. The old days of "red wine goes with red meat (beef, pork, venison, etc.), and white wine goes with white meat (chicken, fish, shellfish, etc.) are forever gone. These days, the correct answer is "whatever your heart desires." Actually, whenever I have salmon steak, I would rather serve it with a glass of light red wine – petite sirah, or Pinot noir.

So, what to do to start learning about wines? Well, first learn about the differences of wines, mainly the red wines and the white wines. As I mentioned earlier, red wines are made with red grapes and white wines with white grapes. Just like there are many kinds of tomatoes – cherry, heirloom, plum, roma, beefsteak ... etc., and it is the same with grapes. For red grapes, there are varieties like Cabernet Sauvignon, Zinfandel, Pinot noir, Gamay Beaujolais, Shiraz, Merlot, Malbec and many others. Each varietal grape has its own flavor and character. But somehow, depending on the region where it is grown, the profile is different from one to the other. Hence, the same grapes that are grown in Napa Valley in California might taste totally different than the grapes that are grown in New Zealand. The climate, the soil and the hours of sunshine everday can make a big difference. As for the whites, there are Chardonnay, Sauvignon Blanc, Semillon, Muscato, Pinot Grigio, Gewurtztraminer, Riesling, and many others. When you look at the label of a wine bottle, you will notice:

The vintner – the vinery that produces that wine – Fetzer, Kendall Jackson, Black Foxcellars, Murphy Goode ...

Vintage – what year was it bottled? 2013, 2009, 1982? Rule of thumb is that the older the bottle, the better the quality because wine improves while aging. That's what they said about women, and my wife agreed totally.

The varietal – what kind of grapes do they use? Pending on different countries, the vintner must use 65 percent to 75 percent of the grapes of what the label states. Hence, if the bottle says Cabernet Sauvignon, it must contain 65 percent to

75 percent of Cabernet Sauvignon grapes, and the others can be a mix of any other grapes.

The country of origin – France, Italy, Germany, California, Argentina, New Zealand ...

So now you have it. But what to do next? Just how do you pick the wine that you like? Well, everyone has his/her own preferences. Some like wines that are full body and heavy, others like it light or a little sweet. The only way to know your wines is that you have to actually taste them. You just can't take someone's words for it just because they said so. I have conducted a wine seminar earlier, and I will share with you a starter chart that you can use. I have chosen five red wines and five white wines, and I listed the name of the wine, how to pronounce it, how it tastes (in general), the regions that they are grown, and a sample food pairing. You can actually start your own chart, and form your own opinion.

I will write more about wines, and share with you my passion and the knowledge I acquired through the years. Have fun. Salute, cheers, skol and gan bay!

Wine tasting 102

S o, have you started your own wine tasting club? It is a good hobby, it is enjoyable, and you always learn something new down the road. There are so many different varietal wines to choose from, and the various regions from which they are harvested. And don't forget, same grapes do taste differently from one country to another. So, just how do we judge the wines we tasted? Furthermore, how do we pick our favorite wines? As I mentioned earlier, let your taste buds make the decisions. Don't let anyone influence you with all the fancy talk, everyone is entitled to their own opinions. And picking your favorite wines is solely your choice. How do you pick your favorite wines? Start small, but think big. Pick a certain wine first, like cabernet sauvignon, find out what you like or don't like about it. And then taste the same wine grown in different countries all over the world. There are cabernet sauvignon wines that are made in France, Italy, the USA, Australia, New Zealand, Argentina, Chile and even China! Follow the chart that I provided, and pick five red wines and five white wines. The red wines are listed from full body to light and delicate. And the white wines are listed from light to sweet. What do you prefer? I personally like cabernet sauvignon as I like that rich, full flavor; but you might prefer something light like Pinot noir. But, you will never know till you have actually tasted them yourself. Took me many years to learn about the fine art of drinking tea, and I have just begun to learn about the fine art of wine drinking, so bear with me.

So, use the wine grading chart that I composed in my college days and record each wine that you have tasted. As the chart grows, so will be your knowledge of different wines.

And you will become a wine expert in no time flat. How do we decide if the wine is good, or well, not so good? Very simple, just follow your eyes (color), nose (bouquet), and taste buds (senses), and grade your wines accordingly.

Appearance – How does it look to you? Is the color rich and attractive?

Aroma – What kind of bouquet do you notice? What does it remind you ... your favorite fruits or flowers?

Body – Is it heavy with substance, or thin and watery?

Taste – How does it feel around your palate? Is it pleasing and delightful? Or is it harsh?

Finish – How does it feel? Does it leave you a sensation that lingers? Is the impression memorable?

There are many terms that are used to describe wines. Don't try to learn them all unless you want to become a wine expert. Know the descriptions so you can relate to others about your experience and can express your impressions easily. It is no point getting into a heated discussion about the terms used, as everyone is entitled to his/her opinion. You might think that particular wine is fruity, while another might think that it is flinty. As long as you are having fun, does it really matter?

The appearance of a wine:

Ruby red – Deep and dark in color.

Clear – Nice transparent color, no sign of any residuals.

Cloudy – Hmmm, don't drink it.

Purplish – Getting there (maturity) but not quite yet.

The aroma of a wine:

Pleasing – We can also use the term "agreeable." It is nice and pleasant.

Bouquet – You smell flowers, fruits, chocolate? What does it remind you of?

Complex – A combination of different sensations – roses and green apples? Fresh mowed lawn? Peaches?

Corky/Musty – Don't drink it. The cork is moldy, and it affects the whole bottle. That's why most vineries these days have switched to twist tops.

Lively – Young and fresh, hasn't aged for very long, yet very pleasant.

Spicy – It has a pleasant kick, a slight bite to it.

BEVERAGES

The body of a wine:
Full body – Rich and dense, it leaves a ring in your glass.
Light body – Thin yet quite pleasant.
Balanced – Not too heavy nor light, medium, compared to being full or light.

The taste of a wine
(How does the wine feel on your palate?):
Acidic – Sign of a new wine – fresh with new harvested fruits.
Fruity – What do you detect? Strawberries, apples, berries?
Flinty – Dry, clean, sharp. It is pleasant, but is it memorable?
Smooth – Perfectly aged.
Sweet – The sugar content is coming through (mostly in Gewurztraminer, Moscato, etc.).
Dry/Crisp – Kind of crisp and puckery, like biting a fresh-picked green apple.
Elegant/Friendly – Distinguishable and yet agreeable.
Balanced – Not too dry or too sweet, just right!
Character – Has the qualities that you will always remember. Friendly – Can go with any dish. And can be consumed any time – before, during and after dinner.
Pleasant – It pleases all senses.
Flavors commingling – You can taste different fruits and spices at the same time.
Bold – Strong and unforgettable.
Warm and Spicy – Let your imagination ride. Zesty – Refreshing, keep you happy.
Abundance – Has plenty more than expected.
Hint of _____ amongst _____ (you fill in the blanks). Leaves flavor of _____ (aftertaste – the finish).
Developing – You can feel the aging process.
Corpulent – Rich, round and full (maturity).
Dense – Heavy and satisfying (not the same in describing a person).

The finish of a wine

Velvety – Nice and smooth, leaving a mellow aftertaste.
Full-bodied – Takes a while to settle in. Heavy and lingers.
Thin – So-so. Not impressive, not worth trying. Rewarding – A memorable experience. It completes your requirement in pleasing all senses.

Now you have it. Just remember, there's no right or wrong descriptions about all the wines you tasted. It is what you think and how you feel about the wine that matters. No one can tell you what you should think or what you should like.

You make that decision. There are many different factors to consider before you become an expert, it will take a while. But meanwhile, just have fun with your journey.

Try wines from different vintage years.

Try wines from different vintners, same region.

Try wines from different countries, same varietal. Learn about wine pairing with foods.

Try different varietal red and white wines. Understand the descriptions and be able to use them appropriately.

Salute, cheers, skol and gan bay!

Wine pairing at Potter's Shed.

Wine seminar at Potter's Shed

I did another wine seminar a few weeks back at the Potter's Shed in Shell Lake. And this time, it was on a much broader scale. We got the Saratoga Liquor Company, a wine distributor, to help us out; and we had over 150 wine lovers who turned out to try 40-plus different wines from countries around the world – Australia/New Zealand, Argentina/Chile, Spain, Italy, France and the U.S. Without spending a fortune, folks could taste the wines from different countries and be able to tell the difference, even if it was from the same varietal grapes. Think about it, if a bottle of wine costs $15, you would have to pay over $600 for all the wines on the display tables.

So, how could the same Cabernet Sauvignon grapes from the Napa Valley in the U.S. taste differently from those that were grown in Australia? An easy, simple and very logical question indeed. Yet, it will take a professional wine connoisseur to explain in detail. And all I can tell you is – one is grown in the Northern Hemisphere, and the other one down South. Fair? The climate is different, and the soil is different; not to mention the aging process. And all that affects the final product.

And the next most popular question was, "What is the difference between a $15 bottle of wine and a $50 bottle of wine; and better yet, a $500 bottle of wine?" I really don't know how to answer that question, as oftentimes, I myself would ask the same. I have tasted wines that cost $200 - $300 or more a bottle. But hate to say, I would not pay that much for a bottle of wine. I like wines that please my taste buds. Many times, the expensive wines do not meet my expectations at all. Maybe I just have less expensive (don't like the word cheap) taste buds to please? Probably. But again, drinking wine is to be able to enjoy it. It is not a competition. If you like the aroma, the taste, the color and the texture of a certain wine, stick with it. But, it will take some time before you find your own prince/princess, so to speak.

So, how much does it cost to produce a bottle of wine? And how do folks like the "Two-Buck Chuck" makers who can sell a bottle of wine for less than three bucks be able to sustain a profit? The answer is volume. To sell 5,000 bottles at a cost of $15 will make you $75,000. With a margin of 5 percent, you make $3,750 profit. But what if you sell 50,000 bottles at a cost of $3? You make $150,000. With the same margin of 5 percent, your profit is $7,500. So, the question remains, who are you? Do you want to have an honorable reputation of being a "classic" wine? Or you just want to make a profit? Trader Joe's carried the wine dubbed "Two-Buck Chuck" for years. I could fill my wine rack for less than $50. Or, should I spend $50 for just one bottle of wine? Again, it is your own preference. What kind of a wine lover are you? After all these years, I am happy that by just taking one sip of the wine, I can tell what varietal it is. Hmmm, is it Gamay Beaujolais? Or maybe Pinot Noir? You have to start somewhere to acquire that knowledge. I am not advising you to start drinking. But hate to say, you have to start somewhere, somehow. Maybe now is the time? No, no, no. I don't mean grabbing just any bottle and drink yourself silly. Start going to wine tasting events and using the chart I composed to grade and record your experience of the wines you have tasted, and you will become a wine expert yourself. What is the appearance? The taste? The aroma? The finish?

And how does it compare to others?

Going back to the costs of a bottle of wine, here is a comparison:

$15 average	$50 average
Cork $.08 (plastic)	$0.41 (natural)
Cap $0.08 (plastic)	$.026 (tin)
Bottle $.0.60 (normal)	$0.80 (heavy)
Label $.20 (plain)	$0.31 (embossed)
Grapes $1.17 (California)	$6.24 (Napa Valley)
$2.13	$8.02

So, just how does Two-Buck Chuck make a profit, selling wines under $3? Again, volume. There is a secret in every trade. So, what is your reputation? Are you a table wine?

Or are you something different? It reminds me of my early days working as a consultant. I have a very good friend that works for a spice company. They make small packages of seasoning for restaurant chains – ketchup and mustard packages; dipping sauces; and the "secret blend" for a fried-chicken chain. I was working with him with a special blend for a BBQ company. And somehow, the name McDonald's came up. And he grunted and shook his head. Being curious, I couldn't help but ask why the long face. Then he explained that McDonald's, being the largest restaurant chain in the world, would take advantage of their buying power. For a certain seasoning blend, the cost may be $1 a pound, and the profit margin might be 5 percent, which is 5 cents per pound. But McDonald's would come in and tell them that they would pay 60 cents a pound instead of a dollar per pound. But they would buy 50,000 pounds at a time. So, instead of making your normal profit, you make much less. But somehow, you turn your idle inventory into floating cash instead.

So, back to the world of selling wines. What other costs are there? Think about it, how much does it cost to fly the wines from Australia or Argentina to the U.S.? And first, they would be stored at the wholesale distributor. Then, who would pay for the transportation? As the distributor has to send them to the individual wine/liquor stores, and then eventually to the restaurants. I don't want to bore you with the figures, but you can do your own calculations. A bottle of wine that might cost $4 might end up costing $40 at a restaurant; which might cost them less than $15 from the distributors. Come to think of it, paying $40 for a bottle of wine (even if it is mediocre) is still a good deal. The owner has to pay for the maintenance, the helpers, the advertising ..., you name it.

So, look for any wine-tasting events, and open your horizons about wines from different countries. Become an expert yourself by knowing the difference of flavors, colors and aromas. Then, learn how to pronounce "Chateauneuf du Pape" without spitting on someone.

TYPICAL WINE CHARACTERS

Name	Pronounciation	Taste	Region	Food Pairing
RED WINES				
Zinfandel	Zin-fan-dell	Heavy and zesty	CA, Italy	Pizza, BBQ
Cabernet Sauvignon	Ca-ber-nay So-vin-yawn	Heavy, full-bodied	CA, Chile, France, Australia	Steaks & chops
Merlot	Mer-lo	Smooth with a hint of fruit - blackberries & plum	Italy, Chile, CA, Australia	Great with anything
Shiraz	Shi-raz	Fruity with a hint of spice	CA, Australia France	Steak & wild games
Pinot Noir	Pee-no no-wah	Delicate & fresh, soft and fruity	France, CA New Zealand	Salmon, chicken, lamb & sushi rolls
WHITE WINES				
Chardonnay	Shar-don-nay	Velvetty with a hint of fruit	CA, Australia Chili	Fish & chicken
Riesling	Rees-ling	Fresh and easy, hint of fresh apples	Germany, CA	Fish, chicken, pork, Asian food
Sauvignon Blanc	So-vin-yawn Blanc	Dry and crisp, a touch of herbal flavor	France, New Zealand	Seafood, salad
Gewurztraminer	Gur-vurtz-tra-meener	Fruity and aromatic, with a hint of spice	Germany, CA, NY	Asian food
Muscato	Mos-cato	Sweet & fruity	Italy, Austria	Great with dessert, or by itself

Wine chart

Mulled wine for the season

How time flies. While we're still enjoying the leftover turkey from the Thanksgiving feast, the Christmas season is approaching fast. As a matter of fact, I'm still working on the Halloween candies. Pretty soon, the radio stations will be playing Christmas music. How jolly can you get with "Jingle Bells" jingling in your head all day long?

I love the holiday season. It is time for sharing, caring and giving. I wish the season would come more often. As much as I don't like the cold weather, I am starting to learn to love everything about living in the cold country. There are so many things to do in the winter. And while we consider it fun and exciting, the southern folks (yes, my family from California) would look at us and say, "What? You do what? Going out and fish on a frozen lake? Are you nuts? What if the ice cracked all of a sudden and you just fall right in?" Ah, a thousand "what ifs" indeed. Yet, year after year, we folks go ice fishing anyway, and cross-country skiing, snowboarding, snowmobiling or just doing nothing but staring out the window, watching the fresh-fallen snow clinging to the window pane, forming snowflakes with a million different designs. And, of course, enjoying a glass of mulled wine while cozying up with your loved one in front of the fireplace is optional, but highly recommended.

I never heard of mulled wine till I started working in the hospitality industry. And it is not till I worked with a restaurant up north that I learn more about this gem. Mulled wine is a European beverage that is "mulled" with different fruits and spices and can be served with or without alcohol. It is served hot or warm in the cold countries. Yet, in Spain, the same drink is served chilled, called sangria (or blood, in translation). Actually, the Romans started serving this concoction during the second century. They brought the recipes to the countries that they conquered and to other countries that they traded with. And, somehow, it caught on, and each country has modified the recipes somewhat and they have created their own formulas.

The recipe is rather simple, it is heated wine that is mixed with fruits and spices. It depends upon different regions and the fruits and spices available, hence all the different guidelines. Mostly the fruits are orange, lemon, lime, apples, berries or even tangerines. And spices include cinnamon, nutmeg, star anise, cloves and ginger. The spices may be combined and boiled in a sugar syrup (or honey) before wine or brandy is added. And talk about adding a hint of fresh holiday scent to your home while the wine is mulling. Biting your tongue, you might wish winter would last a little longer.

So, how to make a perfect mulled wine. Well, forget it, there's no such animal. Just like cooking, there is no recipe that would please everyone. There is always someone who cannot stand certain ingredients. While most of your guests would love what you have created, there will always be a few that find it totally distasteful. So, take their names and cross them off your invitation list next year. Life is simple. Enjoy it with those who share your love and passion.

So, how to mull your wine? Well, set aside the ingredients you need. After a few tries, you will come up with your very own specialty and then name it after you or someone you love. But before your mulling, pick a clean pan/pot that you'll use only in mulling the wine. Do not ever use a regular cooking pan for this mulling purpose, as it will totally ruin the flavor and give it a very disagreeable taste.

So, are you ready to do your own mulling? It is really easy and simple. And once you've mastered your first batch, you're on your way to become a mulling master. As the batch is made up with all different fruits and spices, you do not need to add an expensive wine. I'll cry a thousand tears if you put a bottle of 1945 Rothschild into your recipe. But, of course, if you live in Downton Abbey, be my guest.

Here is one of my creations:

Amery Amy's Merry Nip
Ingredients:
1 bottle red wine
1 orange/tangerine
1/2 cup brandy, vodka or gin (choose one)
2-3 star anise
8-10 whole cloves
2-3 cinnamon sticks
1/2 cup honey

Heat 4 cups of water in your mulling pot; add all spices when boiling. Use your imagination. You can add lemons, limes or cranberries (which are plentiful here in the North Woods) to the batch. Boil for 10 minutes, then turn the heat down and add wine and liquor. If you want it nonalcoholic, just add one quart of apple juice instead.

Again, what makes Amery Amy merry? The trick is, it has to be served hot. And rather than heating the whole batch every time, just microwave each serving for a minute. Add the cinnamon stick and star anise before you set the timer. Trust me, the whole room will be permeated with the holiday scent. Now you have the recipe, adjust the profile to your liking.

Living up here in the North Woods, it seems like everyone is either Norwegian, Danish or Swedish. It is hard for a Chinese guy with gray hair to blend in. But, somehow, I did manage, ha-ha. What wonderful friends they make. I'm counting my blessings every day. Anyway, my Swedish friends taught me a few things about mulling. First, it is called glogg in Swedish, and oftentimes, it is made with fruit juices instead of wine. However, for those who have lived in the North Woods long enough, stronger spirits are added – brandy, vodka or akvavit. And glogg is a popular drink during the Christmas season.

Anyway, don't wait till Christmas to start mulling. Start today and enjoy the season. Who knows? Pretty soon we'll be complaining about the intense summer heat.

Beverage pairing

Iknew nothing about wines till I became a waiter at a
steak house in my senior year in college. The first thing I
learned about wines was – there are red wines, white wines
and rose (or blush wine). You serve red wines with red meat
(steaks, pork or lamb chops) and white wines with white
meat (such as fish and chicken); and rose can be served with
red or white meat. The wine list was filled with names I
couldn't even pronounce. Try "Chateauneuf du Pape" and
repeat it three times. It was very intimidating at first, but
knowing that my tuition came from my tips, I had to make
it my business to be comfortable with those wines so I could
sell them. I read a lot, and I experimented a lot too. There is
no other way, you have to actually taste it and feel it so you
can relate those sensations to your guests. Instead of saying,
"Oh, I don't know, never tried it," I would say, "For your filet
mignon, sir, I would recommend either a glass of Shiraz or
Cabernet Sauvignon. Shiraz is quite fruity and hearty, with a
hint of spice. Cabernet, on the other hand, is full bodied, bold
and rich at the same time." I did manage to pay off my tuition
with the extra tips I made off wine sales.

Know your wines, and the pairing will come easy. Let's
start from the reds:

Malbec (mal-beck) – introduced to the States from the
southern continents – Chile, Argentina and Australia. It is an
easy drinking wine, very mellow and smooth, with a hint of
fruits and spice. Try that with spicy Mexican or Cajun foods.

Merlot (mer-lo) – another easy drinking wine, popular
worldwide. With a "round" texture, it is a great wine for new
wine drinkers. And it goes with most any food.

Cabernet Sauvignon (ca-ber-nay so-vin-yon) – my all-time
favorite! Rich and full bodied, with a hint of dark fruit. Goes
with all red meat.

Shiraz/Syrah (shi-raz or sa-rah) – it is hearty and fruity,
also with a hint of dark fruits. Great with stews, steaks and
wild games.

Pinot Noir (pee-no na-wah) – it is light and fresh, and

quite aromatic. It is not as popular as the other wines as it is quite temperamental; all elements – temperature, sunshine, rain and soil - have to be in perfect condition for growth. But harvest is most worth waiting for. Great with grilled salmon (yes, fish), chicken, lamb and even Japanese cuisine.

Zinfandel (zin-fan-dell) – it is the "heaviest" of all red wines, with a zesty flavor. It originates in Italy, but nowadays most popular in California. Great with pasta and pizzas, especially BBQs.

And let's go with the whites:

Chardonnay (shar-don-nay) – the most popular white wine. Very easygoing, lightly sweet, with a hint of citrus fruits. Great with chicken and seafood.

Riesling (rees-ling) – sweeter in Germany where it originated than those produced in California. It is lighter then Chardonnay, with a hint of fresh fruit and aroma from apples. Great with chicken, seafood, pork dishes and spicy Oriental foods.

Pinot Grigio (pee-no gree-gi-o) – also known as Pinot Gris. It is a bit dry with a nice fruity flavor and aroma. Goes great with seafood and chicken.

Gewurtraminer (ger-wurtz-tra-meener) – slightly sweet with a hint of spice, a good sipping wine. Great with spicy Asian foods.

Moscato (mos-ca-to) – sweet and fruity, with a distinctive aroma. Also, a good sipping wine that goes great with dessert.

Sauvignon Blanc (so-vin-yon blanc) – a dryer wine with flavors from green fruits – apples, pears and gooseberries; and aroma from a freshly mowed lawn. Great with seafood, salads and chicken dishes.

As for the blushes:

We had Mateus and Lancers from Portugal and Spain in the old days. But I can't find them in the market anymore. Rather, the most popular ones are:

White Zinfandel – lightly sweet and aromatic. Even the color is romantic. Pretty much goes great with salads and poultry or fish.

Blush or rose – same.

Of course, there are champagne/bubbling wines and many other varieties of wines, but let's just keep it simple for now.

Even with the same kind of grapes, the taste is a bit different depending on where they are grown, and what year they were harvested. Rain, sunshine and the condition of the soil all contribute to the final texture of the wine. And wine with a higher price tag does not necessary mean that it tastes better than the wines that are cheaper. It is your own preference that counts.

To learn more about wines, I would recommend starting your own wine-tasting club. Pick a wine, red or white, but at a certain price range, say under $20. Select a group of friends (around six) and have each one bring a bottle from a different region with a different vintage year. And have a grading sheet to record the wine according to color, aroma, flavor, texture and the "feel" in your mouth. Serve the wines with cheese and fruits. And then afterward, discuss what you think about each wine. It is fun and educational, and is the best way to experience different wines without spending a fortune. We can talk about wines for weeks and months. But one step at a time. So here, my dear friends, salute, and have fun!

BEVERAGES

The art of tea drinking

My wife loves coffee and I'll make sure that she has a pot of fresh-brewed coffee every morning to start her day. She loves her coffee strong, with a touch of cream to top it off. I can't imagine the success of Starbuck's, all the stuff that they created that made zillions of dollars. I have never heard of "latte" till they came around. And to add a "froth" to the coffee, what in the world is that? When they first opened, everyone laughed, saying that it is the craziest thing. "Selling coffee for 3 bucks or more? When you can get a cup of fresh-brewed coffee at McDonald's for a quarter? You guys will go bankrupt in no time flat," they all said. And here they are, growing bigger and stronger every day. And they were everywhere when we visited China a few years ago. Yes, in China, a tea-drinking country! They haven't invaded this part of Wisconsin yet, thank goodness. But the day will come soon. Meanwhile, I'll stick with my tea.

Tea drinking is an old Chinese tradition that has been around for hundreds and thousands of years. Fable is that the Emperor Shennong (who was the master of herbs and medicines) was away for a bit, while a pot of boiling water was waiting for his return. Somehow, the leaves from the trees fell to the brewing pot, and it added to the accent of the boiling water. The emperor went back for the water to quench his thirst and found that this new flavored water was indeed quite refreshing. And he claimed that henceforth, all water drank should have added flavors with tea leaves for a more pleasant living. And that was 4,200 years ago when it happened.

Yes, everything happens for a reason. Who would ever know that the plant of Camellia sinensis will create such a phenomenon after all these years? I love drinking tea, it is a ritual every morning. After serving my wife her morning coffee, I will boil some water and then brew my own tea. I've learned to be patient, as in my past life of being a business consultant, I was always in a hurry, wanting to know what each situation was, and what I should do to fix the problems.

BEVERAGES

Rush, rush, rush; quick, quick, quick; and fix it now, now, now. However, with my pot of tea, everything changes, no more chop chop. I'll just sit on my porch, watching the birds fly by, and sipping my tea, and go, "ahhhhh." Life is good!

There are many kinds of teas in the market, Oo Long, Dragon Well, Poh Erh and Lychee Red belong to the black tea category. Theh Guan Yin and Jasmine, which belong to the green tea family, are my favorites. And there is another rare gem called Mah Lau Mit (or in translation, Monkey Pick). The monkeys are trained to climb up the cliffs that are difficult for human reach and pick those precious leaves. Those monkeys sure work hard for their keep.

Before you go spend a fortune in getting the proper tea set and taking lessons in tea brewing, just do what I did, start easy and simple. There is a gadget in the market made by Bodum, which is made for brewing coffee. It is a glass jar with a handle that attaches to a steel filter that you can push down. So, boil some water, add two teaspoons of your favorite tea leaves in the jar, and then slowly press down the lever, and patiently wait for a few minutes. Watch the steaming water slowly change color. Pour the tea gently into a white ceramic cup, and smell the aroma. Your first sip is worth a thousand smiles. Took me many years to learn that.

By the way, tea is not just for pleasure drinking. There are many, many rituals in offering tea in China:

When you visit friends at their home, first thing they will offer is some fresh-brewed tea. A way to say, "Welcome to my humble abode." And by golly, no using tea bags, unless that's all you got.

During a ceremony (wedding or birthday), tea is offered to the elders to show respect. The ritual is that we will be on our knees, and then offer the tea above our heads. The elders will then have a sip and then offer a red envelope - lucky pocket money - in return. A good trade indeed.

To offer apologies or forgiveness.

To seal a business deal. No contracts are needed. Millions of dollars of business are done by a tea toast.

In the old days, the young scholars were educated to master the six fine arts – manners, music, archery, humanity, history and mathematics. However; the common folks were keen to the seven necessities of the daily operation of their households – firewood, rice, oil, salt, sauces, vinegar and tea. Your home has to have all those seven ingredients before you can open the door to welcome the day. And tea is one of those that you can't do without.

The British occupied Hong Kong (where I grew up) for many years, and they were known for their afternoon tea with biscuits. Ewww! How one will add sugar and cream to their tea is beyond me. Tea should be drunk as is, with its natural flavor and aroma. There are many teas in the market to choose from, pick and choose your own favorite. It is not an "eat and run" beverage, you have to relax, sit back, and actually taste the flavors. It is an experience. Eat slow, drink slow, enjoy life. I am finally learning what drinking tea is all about. Hope you will too.

CHAPTER FIVE: TRADITIONS

The Chinese New Year

Some of you might not know that the Chinese New Year is coming up soon, next week on Monday, Feb. 8, to be exact. This is going to be the Year of the Monkey; there are 12 animals in the Zodiac calendar and it rotates every 12 years. So, next time the year of the monkey comes around will be in year 2028.

While the Western calendar is based on the movement of the sun, the Chinese lunar calendar is based on the movement of the moon. Where the West has their monthly Zodiac symbols, the Pisces, the Aquarius, the Libra, etc., the East has its own, too, but it goes by annually. Each year is designated to an animal, so if you were born in the Year of the Monkey (1956, '68, '80, '92 and 2004), you are supposed to possess some of the characteristics or traits of a monkey - smart and intelligent, creative and inventive, but have little patience and can be easily discouraged. Good companions are those born in the Year of the Dragon, but avoid the tiger! Well, I am a tiger and I am supposed to be aggressive and courageous, yet stubborn with a fighting spirit and never give up easily. A horse or dog will make a good companion, but avoid the monkey. Interesting facts, indeed, but let's talk about the events in Chinese New Year.

Growing up in Hong Kong, Chinese New Year was the biggest event of the whole year, and the fun lasted for weeks!

As New Year is approaching, the "New" applies to everything; it is a new beginning, a new fresh start and everyone prays that it will bring peace, joy, health and prosperity to self, friends and families. Before the official New Year Day comes, families will spend days cleaning and tidying up their homes. Fresh flowers would be displayed everywhere. Family members who have been away for school or business would return to their homes to have the family gathering meal in welcoming the new year. I remember fondly that:

- We will have new shoes and clothing to start the year.
- My mother, my aunts and Pao Pao (grandma) would spend days cooking a bunch of fun foods, foods that rhyme with the Chinese words for "good fortune," for us to munch on.
- We would have banquets after banquets to welcome the new year, serving foods that also symbolized good fortune.
- Firecrackers would be setting off before sunrise. They are banned these days as a lot of young kids set them off carelessly and caused many unnecessary accidents. Hearing them cracking in the loudspeakers just isn't the same.
- This is the time to pay respect to the elders. The streets would be filled with families visiting their elders to wish them the best. Taxis would triple their normal fares but no one complained.
- My all-time favorite was pocket money stuffed in a red envelope. Elders are supposed to give pocket money to the young ones as they pay respect. After a day of visiting elderly uncles and aunts, I would have enough "loot" to play with for weeks.
- Red and gold are lucky colors and banners with the lucky colors would be displayed everywhere – in shops, markets, homes, town halls, restaurants and even in churches.
- Greet each other with "Kung hey fat choy" (Wish you become prosperous) every place you go. Or these days, in Mandarin, "Kung xi far chai."

All those have become fond memories. I don't really see any festive displays here unless I am in Chinatown in California or Toronto. Regardless, kung hey fat choy, my dear friends - happy Year of the Monkey. Wish you all stay healthy, wealthy, and may all your troubles and worries be left behind.

Happy Cinco de Mayo

This Thursday is Cinco de Mayo, the fifth of May, a big day of celebration for our Mexican friends. A lot of folks think that Cinco de Mayo is the Mexican Independence Day, just like the Fourth of July. It is a day of celebration, with parades marching down Main Street, mariachi music blasting in most Mexican restaurants and street festivals! However, there are only a few towns in Mexico that celebrate Cinco de Mayo. Mexican Independence Day is on Sept. 16, so what is this big hoopla about Cinco de Mayo? To tell the truth, it is a holiday created by the beer and tequila companies. Go to any Mexican restaurants on that day, I guarantee that you'll see red, green and white, which are Mexican national colors, colored banners hanging from ceiling to ceiling. I bet that for every three or four flags there will be one flag with a beer or tequila logo on it. Si, viva Corona, Dos Equis (yes, long live Corona, Dos Equis – beer companies); viva Cuervo Gold, Don Pedron (long live Cuervo Gold, Don Pedron – tequila companies)! No one ever remembers that on May 5, 1862, in the town of Puebla, Mexico, the outnumbered Mexican army, which was made up of mostly farmers and common folks, defeated the heavily armed French army, and stopped the French from colonizing Mexico. So, forget about the beer and tequila companies for a while and have a toast to the true heroes behind Cinco de Mayo.

How do we do our own celebration? First, let's start with making some margaritas. The easiest way to make margaritas is to mix tequila and triple sec with some sweet and sour (lime) juice. Tequila is made with blue agave plant in the city of Tequila, a region of Jalisco, Mexico. There are three grades of tequila, silver is fresh from the distillery drum; gold has been aged in wooden barrels for at least six to 18 months; and anejo, which has been aged from three to six years and is much smoother and more expensive. Triple sec is an orange liqueur. Most sweet and sour juices are just plain lime juice with added sugar. A can of frozen lime juice in the market costs less than $2, but the bottled one with a known brand name attached costs $5 or more. So, it's your choice.

You can serve a margarita on the rocks - over ice, or blended - mixed in the blender. Either way, it is refreshing. For each serving add 1 oz. of tequila and a half oz. triple sec, with 4 oz. of sweet and sour. Pour it into a margarita salt-rimmed glass with a lime wheel for garnish. Trust me, you'll be the hero. To get a perfect lime wheel, take a fresh lime and remove both ends. Then make a small cut lengthwise, about half an inch, and then simply slice across. The wheels that come out will have an opening that just fits over the glass. There are special margarita glasses just for the drink but a wine glass will fit the purpose. Now, to be creative you can make margaritas with different fruits. The best ones are with fresh strawberries or with some fresh mangos. First, put the fruits in a blender, then add your margarita and blend it again with the fruits. There you have it, a fresh homemade strawberry or mango margarita. Be sure to try other fruits with the blended strawberries or mango. The list can go on and on, and your enjoyment lingers.

Now you've a margarita in one hand, your other hand should be busy with chips and salsa - or better yet, with some fresh-made guacamole.

Pico de Gallo, "Salsa Fresca" *Serves eight*
Ingredients:
- 6 Roma tomatoes with the seeds removed
- 2 stalks of celery, diced
- 1 jalapeno, finely diced
- 1 red onion, finely diced
- 1 cup cilantro, finely chopped
- 1 lime's worth of juice
- 1 tsp. garlic salt

In large bowl mix ingredients well. Adjust flavor to taste. Add more garlic salt and/or lime juice for a stronger taste.

Pico de Gallo means the beak of a rooster. It is pronounced "pea-ko de guy-yo."

Guacamole *Serves eight*
Ingredients:
- 4-6 soft avocados
- 1 tomato, diced
- 1/4 cup red onion, finely diced
- 1/2 cup cilantro, finely chopped
- 1 lime, juiced
- 1/2 jalapeno, finely chopped (optional)
- 1 tsp garlic salt

In large bowl, add avocados that have their skin and pits removed. Add the rest of ingredients and mash till pulpy. Only use jalapeno if you like the hot and spicy kick. You can serve guacamole lumpy or smooth, which will require more mashing. Again, season to taste. Get the tortilla chips that won't break when you dip into the mix.

What are you waiting for? Summer is not that far away and it is time to practice now for that perfect margarita party in your backyard. Remember: practice, practice and more practice. Happy Cinco de Mayo, mis amigos!

Kung Hei Fat Choi– Happy New Year

The 28th of this month is the beginning date of the Chinese New Year. The Chinese goes by the lunar calendar, hence the New Year falls on different dates each year. This is the year of the rooster, guess that would make Colonel Sanders happy. There are twelve animals to the zodiac calendar, which rotates every twelve years. If you were born in 1969, 1981, 1993 or 2005, you are a rooster. And there will be the rat, ox, tiger, rabbit, dragon, snake, horse, sheep, monkey, dog and boar. Each animal has their trait of personalities and characters that either match up or clash with other animals. I never believed that until I read the placemat in a Chinese restaurant.

Born under the sign of the rooster, one is supposed to be honest, energetic, flexible, flamboyant, confident, resourceful and a bit arrogant. Well, I was born under the sign of a tiger but I feel that there is a bit of rooster in me. Well, except being flamboyant and arrogant, you can tell from the clothes I wear.

Lunar New Year is the most important festival of all. It is a new beginning, a fresh start with new hopes and promises for a brighter future. Every household would do what it takes to welcome the new year, including cleaning the house from top to bottom, decorating it with miniature tangerine trees or peach blossoms and, of course, the narcissus flowers which, somehow, blossoms only during the lunar months. Their fragrance brings such a welcoming touch to the households.

As kids, we looked forward to the New Year festivities every year. We would get new clothes, new shoes and plenty of "red pocket money" from our elders. There would be lion dance and dragon dance on the streets, with firecrackers crackling everywhere. I think they have banned firecrackers these days, as it caused a lot of unnecessary accidents when kids would go after the firecrackers that hadn't popped, just to find out that they would later as they had a slow fuse. Many people lost their eyesight and fingers because of that. So, these days, the crackling fireworks could be heard only from loudspeakers set up on the street corners instead. Also, there are now no fumes that could choke you for days.

It is a new beginning for all, new clothes, new shoes and a new haircut. On New Year's Eve, there would be a long line waiting at the barbershop. It is a bad omen to get a haircut during the New Year. "Hair" rhymes with "prosperity." How dare one want to get rid of prosperity with the upcoming new year? Besides all the rituals, foods were our major concern. On New Year's Eve, all traveling family members are expected to be home to enjoy the feast together. Just like the Southerners eat black-eyed peas and collard greens for good luck, the Chinese have many lucky foods at a New Year feast. The Chinese are very superstitious, and all the lucky foods rhyme with something that means good fortune or prosperity. How dare me to question that.

So, are you ready to follow the ritual? If that means that will bring you good fortune or prosperity, why take a chance?

• Tangerines rhymes with gold, so eat plenty of them, but don't arrange them by fours in a bowl as four rhymes with death.

• Eat a lot of noodles, it brings longevity.

• Whole fish served head to tail (yes, you learn to enjoy the fish eyeball). Fish rhymes with leftovers. Think about your bank account.

• Long string beans, again, long life.

• Candy tray with eight treats, as eight rhymes with prosperity. Roasted melon seeds, sugar-coated lotus roots, ginger and coconuts are popular choices.

• Dumplings or pot stickers look like a bursting purse or an old gold bar. A must-have for the new year.

• Lettuce rhymes with generating fortune.

• Pork/duck tongue, tongue rhymes with profit. Be brave and make money. I have to dare you to try duck tongues some day.

• Dried oysters rhymes with good market. Can you imagine a dish with lettuce and dried oysters? "Good market that generates a fortune."

The Chinese New Year celebration lasts 15 days. While spending weeks to prepare for the new year, folks would spend each day for two weeks to celebrate the significance of each New Year's day. As a kid, my most fond memory was the red pocket money, as it was pocket money that was mine to own. We got pocket money during the New Year, birthdays and whatever special occasions. I remember that during the New Year, most businesses would be closed for four days, except restaurants, as that would be their busiest time. My parents would lead us to pay respect to our elders, who would patiently wait in their apartments for the younger ones to pay respect to them. We couldn't take the bus or the tram, as long lines would formulate and it would take hours to hop on. So, we would take the local taxis. Their meters were down already, not charging the regular fee. My father would pay whatever the driver demanded, and around the city we went, just to pay respect to the elders. For three days we would be doing that, and all I can remember was counting the loot at the end of the day with my younger brother. Oh, how I remember the generous relatives and those who were not so generous.

Like the rituals of Thanksgiving here in the states, the New Year's feast resembles that a lot, being thankful for family getting together, and hoping and praying that the New Year would bring every one of us wealth, health and prosperity. And most important, peace to all.

Kung Hei Fat Choi to all!

CHAPTER SIX: KITCHEN SETUP

A wittle bit more wok and roll

So, you didn't spend thousands of dollars remodeling the kitchen, and then hundreds more in acquiring fancy gadgets. Did you? Please say you didn't. Yes, you want to get the best equipment (especially knives) so you can get the job done more effectively and efficiently. Yet I have never heard of folks buying kitchen supplies as an investment, and getting rich after many years keeping them in mint condition.

Being Chinese, I love to hear when folks tell me that they like Chinese food. But when I asked them what kind of Chinese food that they fancy, they would give me that blank look and said "uh, what?" I would be a bit irritated at the beginning. But then, as I spent more and more time studying foods from different regions in different countries, I began to realize (but never will admit) just how dumb that question was.

So, let's keep our focus on Chinese foods, shall we? We see restaurants claiming that they specialize in cuisines from certain regions of China – Cantonese, Shanghai, Szechuan, Hunan, Peking and even Mongolia. So, what's the difference? Remember my motto of "make do with what you got"? Well, that's what it is all about.

Hong Kong and Canton (also known as Guang Tung or Guang Chau) are located on the southern tip of China. Being next to the coast and close to the ocean, seafood is plentiful. Vegetables and fruits love growing in this tropical region. And rice is a steady daily staple. Most dishes are just lightly seasoned, steamed or quick stir-fried. Chefs are challenged to create dishes that are simple yet elegant. Dim sum houses are very popular here. Dim sum (touch of the heart) is served steaming hot on pushcarts. These are tiny appetizers, bite size, which are steamed, deep-fried or whatever the chef fancied. There are hundreds of varieties. Most dim sum houses are packed on weekends, when families can get together and exchange stories of their daily accomplishments. There are no menus on the table. You pick out what you want when the carts pass by, and the server adds up how many dishes you had when you're done, and that's your bill. Another tradition of dim sum houses is that they always serve you tea of the highest quality (no wonder, most of them charge $1 per head). There are many rules that we observe in the dim sum houses. Let's talk about them later.

On the west are the regions of Szechuan, Hunan and Yunnan. Because of the raging rivers flowing all year long in the area, and with the high mountains surrounding the area, the weather is cold and damp in winter and hot, muggy and steamy in summer. Red chilies are added to most all dishes. Rice is abundant but not as in demand as in the south. To Fu (made from soybeans) are most popular here. And you will find the ingredients of a lot of products are made of soybeans – soy milk, soy wrappers, soy beans, buns with sweet soy paste..., you name it. "Ma Pao To Fu" is served in most Szechuan restaurants. Legend says that many years ago, a disfigured widow with pimpled face had a tiny roadside café serving the travelers. She had only one entrée to serve – Braised To Fu. But she would serve it the way as requested – more spice, more aroma, more heat ... the way you expected. Her Braised To Fu became so popular that the customers would name it after her.

Farther north is Beijing (Peking), the capital of China. The north is not known for its foods. Muttons and pork are popular, and chickens are raised for their eggs by the poor. Only on special occasions would wealthy families put chicken on their menu. Duck, however, is a different story. Actually, most Peking duck is served three ways, and the crispy skin is the main attraction:

The crispy skins are carefully sliced off the perfectly roasted duck. Then the skins are served in small, puffy pancakes with scallions and a dash of plum sauce.

The meats are taken off the bone, and stir-fried with vegetables.

The bones are used to make a soup.

There are no rice fields in the north, but wheat fields are plentiful. Hence, no rice; but lots of flour for noodles, pancakes, dumplings and steamed buns. Most vegetables used are fermented or pickled cabbage and mustard greens harvested in summer. A lot of animal fats are added to the dish. Garlic, leeks and chilies are used in most dishes, and sauces are made with fermented black beans and soy beans.

On the east sits Shanghai, another seaport that is vital to the trading business of China. The great Yangtze River rages from the west and ends up merging with the mighty ocean in the east. Hence, Shanghai is mostly famous for its seafood dishes and other delicacies. Sauces are known to be heavy, pungent and plentiful. One can always taste the hint of rice wine and the sweetness from the dark cane sugar.

My favorite Siu Long Bau is so very delicate and tasty. Those are steamed buns served in a bamboo steamer. You have to use the spoon to dish it out carefully from the container. Otherwise, the skin would break, and you would have the soup (juice) all over the table.

And the dipping sauce is another story. One must use finely sliced ginger, with a touch of vinegar.

I've written an article earlier on making pot stickers (Wor Tehr) with ground turkey for Thanksgiving. We can talk about that again later.

Food safety in our kitchen

I have taught food sanitation for many years. Yes, it is extremely important for hospitality institutions to follow all the rules and regulations in order to serve foods that are safe for the public. It is mind-boggling to see that many times, even though the safety rules are not followed, luckily, nothing ever happens. However, sometimes a minor incident can lead to a major disaster.

I lived in San Diego for many years; it is my old stomping ground since my college days. I remember that there was a restaurant called Gulliver's back in the '70s. They specialized in serving prime rib, and folks were willing to wait an hour for a table. Remember Gulliver the traveler, who ventured to the lands with giants and then the land with small people? All the settings and costumes in the restaurant were designed to revive your imagination. It was the place to be, and it was one of the most popular restaurants in town. Then, one day, disaster hit. A customer called the health department and complained that he got sick after dining at the restaurant. Upon investigation, the health department found that one of the cooks had been infected with hepatitis A, which is transmitted from feces of people or contaminated seafood. It was a simple safety issue which could be corrected immediately. However, the manager in charge was arrogant and refused to work with the health inspector in addressing those issues. So, the health inspector filed a report and sent a message to the local media, announcing that any customer who had dined at the restaurant within a certain period had to go to the nearest hospital for a medical checkup to ensure that they did not contract hepatitis A and so that they would not infect others around them. The whole city was in a turmoil, as everyone was in fear of being infected. And guess what happened to the business? It went downhill and never recovered. Last time when I visited San Diego, the once-popular restaurant was plowed down and was replaced by a hotel instead. A sad, but true, story.

A lot of us don't pay much attention in our own homes,

thinking that bad things only happen in restaurants. Not true at all. Folks get sick not only by eating spoiled foods, but it can also be caused by many other factors:

• Contaminated by household chemicals. Do not set bleach or ammonia, or any cleaning agent next to food items; store them in a place away from food items. Do not ever mix ammonia and bleach together, it creates a poisonous fume that can cause death!

• Physical materials such as staples from boxes, broken glass, hair, bandages and bones.

• Foods not fully cooked, especially chicken, which can carry salmonella, and raw hamburger, which can carry E. coli.

• Foods not held properly. Cold foods that are held under 40 degrees Fahrenheit and hot foods that are held above 140 degrees Fahrenheit are considered safe. Anything in between is considered dangerous, as bacteria multiply by the millions between 40 F and 140 F degrees. This is the danger zone. So, eating an egg sandwich that has been left on the counter for two to three hours at room temperature can mean disaster!

• Using contaminated utensils: that can be the knives, the cutting board, or the towel that we use. Think about it; using the same knife that we just finished cutting raw chicken with to slice an apple. Or, using the same cutting board to cut lettuce after using the board to make hamburger patties. That's called cross-contamination. And it is the root of many food-poisoning incidents.

Sizzler was once a very popular restaurant chain, with restaurants in different states and even in foreign countries. And because of a minor cross-contamination incident, the chain no longer exists. It is another true, but sad, story. A little girl got sick and died after eating a salad at one of the Sizzler restaurants. Later, they found out that the lettuce from the salad had been contaminated. While the lettuce was being washed in a prep sink, another prep cook was making hamburger patties right next to the sink. Somehow, a small bit of hamburger meat fell into the prep sink. No big deal, right? But, that small piece of hamburger meat was contaminated with E. coli bacteria that can make people sick. When cooked properly, it would be fine. However, the whole batch of salad was contaminated by one little piece of hamburger meat. After eating the salad, the little girl felt violently ill, and she died not long afterward. The parents were devastated, as that little girl was their miracle child. The restaurant had been warned by the health department before but did nothing to prevent further incidents. A big lawsuit followed and the chain disappeared, all because of one incident. No matter how large the compensation was, it could not replace the loss of a precious life.

Bacteria are harmful microorganisms that live amongst us. Those that prompt sickness are harmful but others can be beneficial, such as the yeasts we use in making bread and brewing beer. I will write more on sanitation standards. But meanwhile, start creating a sanitized environment in your own kitchen:

• Cook food properly. Use a food thermometer to ensure that the meat is cooked at the right temperature: seafood, eggs and steaks at 145 F; hamburger, ham and roasts at 155 F; and chicken, turkey and stuffing at 165 F.

• Wash your hands with soap and hot water before, during and after prepping food.

• Sanitize your knives and cutting board after prepping each item. Prep vegetables and fruits first, then meat items afterward to prevent cross-contamination.

• Be aware of the danger zone between 40 F and 140 F. Never leave food within the danger zone, as bacteria multiply by the millions within a second.

Good luck. Stay healthy and be happy.

Food safety in the kitchen, part 2

In the hospitality industry, a negative announcement from the health department spells disaster. If a customer or employee becomes sick at your restaurant, guests will stop coming immediately. Not too long ago, there was a Mexican restaurant chain in Minneapolis that had a problem with food contamination. It was not any fault of the production process of the restaurant, but rather, a problem with the grower. Yet, someone got sick from eating the food from the restaurant, and that's all it takes. Sales plummeted, and they are still trying to find ways to rebuild their image.

Yes, it's no fun being labeled unsafe by the health department. Customers stop coming, which means that there are no sales. And owners know what that means, no income, yet bills keep piling up. What to do? It will take a long time to recuperate from the negative publicity, with the use of lots of goodwill and promotions. And how about the potential lawsuits? You are being sued for negligence while you have done everything you possibly can to provide a clean and safe working environment. And the insurance rate will go up immediately. Not to mention the bad rap amongst the community. Folks will tell five friends about their pleasant dining experience; but will tell 15 or more friends about their not-so-pleasant ones. Employees morale will definitely go down. And with no guests, ever, the business will eventually close. No business, no profits, no jobs. No joke!

We've talked about food safety issues in restaurants earlier, but what about in our own kitchens? Well, let's just follow the same restaurant guidelines and play it safe:

• Purchasing – shop smart, don't buy the products on sale which are past their expiration dates. I once purchased packages of cheese on sale, just to find out that there were black molds on the back and I had to discard them. Saved a few pennies, lost more dollars.

• Storage – don't pack raw chicken and vegetables next to each other on the same shelf. Prevent cross-contamination by grouping foods on different shelves. Those that can cause contaminations should be separate from vegetables and fruits. Keep your household cleaners away from food. Put them under the sink or inside a closet.

• Prepping – again, using cutting boards that are washable with no cracks that could harbor bacteria. Sanitize the board after each use. Cut vegetables first and meat products last. And, of course, wash your hands properly. How long should you wash your hands with soap under running water? Sing "Happy Birthday" from start to finish and you're set.

• Cooking – time to invest in a thermometer and cook food to the right temperature. Notice that many restaurants do not serve rare hamburgers anymore. They are served medium well, which is over 155 F. The temperature for chicken and turkey stuffing should be 165 F. A family got sick after their Thanksgiving dinner and had to spend the evening at the emergency room, just to find out that the problem was caused by eating the stuffing, which was not cooked properly.

• Cleaning – sanitize the knife and cutting board after each use. Wipe the counter with sanitizer such as vinegar and water to keep bacteria from building. A clean counter might look pretty as it is clean and shining, but a sanitized counter is bacteria free.

• Serving – serve hot food hot, above 140 F, and cold food cold, under 40 F. Anything in between is called the danger zone. Eating egg salad or a fish sandwich that has been left out for hours on the counter spells disaster.

There are many kinds of bacteria that can make people sick. The most common kinds are E. coli, from raw ground beef and contaminated produce; botulism, from baked potatoes and improperly canned food; and salmonella, from raw chicken and eggs. And, of course, there are parasites that live in fish and produce. The most common ones are molds, which are found in jams, jellies, ham and bacon, and yeasts, which grow in acidic food with little moisture. It smells or tastes like alcohol and can spoil food quickly.

All these harmful bacteria (microorganisms, or pathogens) will multiply by millions under these conditions. We call it FAT TOM, which stands for food, acid, temperature, time, oxygen and moisture. Leave a piece of cheese on your counter for a few days and see for yourself what happens.

There is another restaurant procedure that we should use at our homes. It is called the first-in-first-out method. How many times do we notice a foul odor when we open our refrigerator just to find out that there is something unrecognizable hiding in the back? FIFO will eliminate that problem. It's simple. Before we put new items in our refrigerator, freezer or the pantry, we move the old items to the front and then put the new items in the back. So now we can see the old items in the front and will use them first. No chance of any food molding and getting spoiled. The restaurants use this method for their foods and beverages too. Remember some time ago, Budweiser was promoting the beers with birth dates? They have supervisors who go around to different bars and test the beers to make sure that they are not "skunky." What a job! I tried to apply for the position and they put me on a 20-year waiting list. So, all restaurants and bars have to practice FIFO with their inventory. We are all human, and sometimes it is just easier to replace the empty slots than to move all the old bottles to the front and put the new ones all the way to the back. With the birth date on the bottle, there's no place to hide. Clever idea, indeed.

Summer is here, and our garden is loading up with zucchinis and cucumbers. I have some recipes that I would love to share with you. Meanwhile, eat well and stay healthy.

CHAPTER SEVEN: LIFE

Time to start Wok and Rolling

Can't believe that I've been writing this column for over a year now. Don't even remember how it got started, but it has been a good journey. Having strangers greet me every place I go is such an honor and surprise. "Hey, are you that (gray-haired Chinese) guy that writes the article in the Leader?" "Yes, I am Peter Kwong, nice to meet you." "I like what you wrote, you're funny. Keep it up." "Well, thank you very much," I said, "I'll keep doing my best." How life is full of funny turns. Never dreamt that I'd be teaching cooking classes, not to mention writing a weekly column.

Very strange indeed, as I've never lifted a finger in the kitchen while growing up in Hong Kong. My family wasn't rich, but somehow did manage to hire an amah to help out with the daily household chores; as my mother had to help out with my Kung Kung (grandpa on my mother's side's) grocery business. Yes, life was good then. I would find my place at the dining table when they yelled, "Dinner is ready." And afterward, would go about with my daily routine. No worries about doing dishes or cleaning up. However, after coming to the States, my whole world turned upside down. I got my first job as a dishwasher in a small Chinese restaurant to supplement my tuition. It was a rude awakening – cleaning pots and pans that the chef left after a long day of cooking. I went to class with blistered fingers for weeks. Could barely hold a pencil or use the typewriter (remember that old gismo with ribbons and pounding keys). But how the cooking journey began.

I was promoted to be a prep cook soon, then the line cook (or wok chef). Later, I started working in a fancy steakhouse as a server. That's the time when I had to learn about wine pairing, and all those fancy names – the vintage and vintners and all that. A big challenge indeed for a college boy who only drank cheap beers. Regardless, after a decade or two working in the hospitality industry for big corporations, I decided to spin out and work on my own as a consultant. After many years of traveling - setting the menus for different concepts, choosing the proper cooking equipment, and creating recipes and training the staff, I decided to settle down and be an instructor instead. Did that for a few years, have turned my head many times when someone addressed me as "Professor Kwong" or "Chef Peter." "Who, me?" I wondered. "Oh yes, that's me." I would then acknowledge that with a smile.

Yes, without a single doubt, cooking is not for everyone. First, you have to plan the menu, then the shopping, the prepping, the cooking, the table setting, and finally the cleaning up, ugh! But then, why would our grandmas do it year after year, with a smile? You go figure. And when the words "love," "joy" or " fun" and "togetherness" are mentioned, then Bingo – does the word "happiness" comes to mind too? That's what cooking is all about.

Yes, when it comes to cooking, fear sets in, especially for those who have never held a sharp object (called a knife) in his/her hand. But we've got to eat every day. And if Big Mac is your answer, read no further. But, don't let Ronald McDonald command your diet, how about some KFC chicken? No, I'm just kidding. There is Arby's nearby. Or DQ? Chilled and grilled, how romantic. But, ask yourself, are you ready to move on? Creating something healthy and delicious and costs little? You've to make the decisions.

I love Julia Child. She is such an inspiration to all of us chefs. She became an expert in French cooking not knowing anything about cooking to start with. You can read more about her stories, but I just want to capture her spirit about her cooking success. And these are my thoughts in paving your way in becoming the master in your own kitchen:

• Learn the basics – how to set up your kitchen. The cutting board, the knives you need, and all other utensils or gadgets that are a must to have. The storage (refrigerator), the wash area (the sink), the prep area (the cutting boards), and cooking area (the stoves and fryers) are all in arm's reach.

• The knife skills that you need, how to hold a knife, and how to chop, slice, dice and mince. The knife works both ways, it can be a great tool, or cut you if you are not careful. So, learn how to master the skills, and use the knife to your advantage. Forget about all these fancy gadgets. A sharp knife is all you need.

• The spices you needed – stock your pantry with basic spices and ingredients you need, but not everything in the market.

• Cooking methods: Stir-fried, deep-fried, braised, stewed, steamed, sautéed or pan fried; what does it mean for each procedure? And what would the end product taste like?

• The necessary sauces – either homemade or purchased.

• Plate presentation – how would your entree/appetizer look on a platter? Use your imagination.

I emphasize on three elements of utilizing your senses to judge an entree:

• How does it look (with your eyes) – the colors of the ingredients?

• How does it smell (with your nose) – the herbs and spices.

• How does it taste – can you detect the five flavors (sweet, sour, bitter, spicy and saltiness) in the ingredients?

So, are you ready to Wok and Roll? Yes, the first step is the hardest – where to go and what to do? I offer different cooking, Chinese, Mexican and Italian, classes all over, just call your local school district's community education office and enquire about the schedules. No, we don't need fancy gadgets or fancy equipment (a 30,000 BTU stove) to cook a delicious meal. Put your heart in the right place, everything is possible.

Yes, start Wok and Rolling, a good start to find happiness.

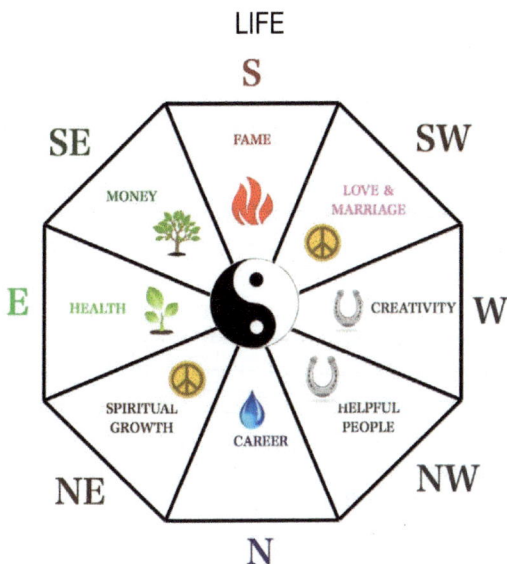

LIFE

S

SE — MONEY — FAME

SW — LOVE & MARRIAGE

E — HEALTH

W — CREATIVITY

NE — SPIRITUAL GROWTH — CAREER — HELPFUL PEOPLE

NW

N

Feng shui

When I was a restaurant consultant in Milwaukee, I helped a lot of restaurants fix their operation problems. Often the question was, "Why are the restaurants not making a profit?" Of course, there are hundreds and thousands of reasons why – location, price, service, cleanliness – but mainly, it goes to the root of all problems: Do we have the right concept serving the food that the public wants? And is the restaurant set up properly so it can operate effectively and efficiently? Without consciously knowing much about feng shui, I was actually using the principles of feng shui in coming up with different logical solutions.

So, what is feng shui? Growing up in Hong Kong, that term came up constantly. In straight translation, "feng" is wind, and "shui" is water. Hence, the directions of how and where the wind and water are flowing affect one's future. The folks in Hong Kong are dead serious about feng shui, and many feng shui masters are consulted before the construction of a building or picking a grave site to bury their elders. And the most common ones are to make sure that their own home carries a good feng shui flow.

I remember a story about a local bank that wanted to move to a new location, and they consulted a feng shui master to approve the blueprint, just to make sure that all elements were in harmony. And, lo and behold, everything guaranteed a prosperous future except that the front entrance, which was facing the Main Street with the rails of the running trams, was considered to be bad feng shui, as it was too busy and disruptive, and might disturb the future peace and harmony of the business. And guess what the bank did. They actually altered the front entrance so it would not face directly to the main road but sideways. Yes, in this day and age, one word from the master, and they would rather spend hundreds and thousands of extra dollars to ensure a prosperous future. And after all these years, business is now better than expected, with no incidents or accidents. So, who's to believe?

Feng shui is the study of the heavens and the Earth in relation to humans. It has been around since the Qin Dynasty, the first emperor of China 221- 207 B.C. It is the theory of five natural elements, metal, wood, water, fire and earth, and how they coexist in harmony and create a balance in the universe. The metal, in the form of an ax or a saw, can destroy a forest.

Yet, trees can stop a flood, but a fire can wipe out a forest. While fire can be put out by rain and the earth can slow down or even stop a flood, more so, the precious metals are hidden under the soil until they are unearthed. It is a balance of destruction and creation, all under the name of harmony.

I love to cook, and my kitchen has to have that flow of energy and efficiency. It is the same principal that I used with commercial kitchens. There are five elements to consider when we design a kitchen: how much food to bring in, where to store it, where to prepare it, where to cook it and how to serve it properly. It has to have that flow, which I call "work flow." Can you imagine if you have to run back and forth to get the food from storage, then prep it on one end of the kitchen, just to run to the other end to store it? You catch my drift. And imagine all the unnecessary accidents that could happen. And the same applies to the front house. To see a server run around taking my order, just to run to the other end to ring it up, and to then run to the kitchen to get the food just drives me nuts!

And to see some restaurants actually have their rest rooms designed to face the dining room. Eew! I'll say no more.

I teach about yin and yang with my cooking – the balance of colors, flavors and aromas that intrigue our senses. Instead of looking at just red or green, how about adding some white, yellow or colors of different shades. And instead of just sweet or salty, how about a different sensation of sweet and sour? Folks love German potato salads, or sweet and sour pork for that reason. Yin is the feminine side of the elements – soft, dark, still, passive, blue and green in colors, the empty spaces and the curves. The yang is the masculine side – hard, bright, moving, active, warm red tones, the solid structure and the geometric lines. It is the balance of yin and yang that gives harmony in the surroundings.

Just as the restaurant needs a good work flow, our household needs the same, which we call chi. It is the energy flow that makes us feel good and refreshed. It is important to keep a good flow of chi in our home. Too much or not enough flow is unhealthy. Think of a healthy river or lake. Too much water flow can cause a flood or eroding of the riverbanks. And stagnant water is worse, as insects will start to infest, and the stench is unbearable. With all that information, you can create your own healthy feng shui, how to keep the healthy air circulating in your house and how to keep the warm sunshine permeating your home. In feng shui, there are a lot of rules and guidelines, but you can simplify the process. Just do it from your heart, and use your common sense. Put hanging plants in windows that are too bright; put lights in corners that are too dark; avoid placing tables and chairs with sharp corners on paths that you can run into; or place an aquarium or a small water fountain in corners that need some life or movement. Follow your heart, and do whatever you feel is comfortable and natural; the positive chi will follow. Have some fun and good luck.

Pet fish

My wife loves animals and I just like to cook them. Out of respect, I will not make roast duck, rack of lamb, frog legs, venison or rabbit stew at home. Heaven forbid we have Bambi and Thumper for supper. However, I might order them when we go out to dinner and she won't even look at me when I am devouring my favorites.

While living in Milwaukee, we had three cats, seven birds and three tanks of tropical fish; thank goodness we have downsized. She loves her cats, so every time when I use the phrase "there are many ways to skin a cat," I have to make sure that she is not around. I do not hate cats but it is just annoying knowing that all they do, besides eating and sleeping, is shed their fur, poop and pee in odd places excluding their litter boxes, use our expensive couch as their scratching post and produce an occasional hairball, which always find ways to my bare foot. I stopped complaining, as the only thing she would always say is "But honey, they are so cute." What to say and what to do?

I find comfort with my tank of tropical fish, they are my true pride and joy; easy to maintain and no pooping and peeing in odd places. I change the water every six or seven months, scrub inside the tank occasionally to clean the moss buildup and that's it. While the cat food and kitty litter would cost more than my beer, a container of fish food costs less than $3 and lasts more than a month. You do the math!

Growing up in Hong Kong, I always loved pet fish. Goldfish, tetras, angel fish and neons, I found it soothing and peaceful just watching them swim around. I never had a tank until we finally moved into our own apartment, living by ourselves with no other families. I don't remember how I learned about setting up. I saved up enough money to get a good-sized tank, 3'x1.5'. It set nicely on top of our china cabinet. There was a pet fish store closed by and I always asked the owner a lot of questions. He was kind enough to tell me what equipment I would need, teach me about different fish behavior and how to maintain the water condition. He had good advice and a great strategy to get me hooked. I can still see the smile in his face, I was a great customer for life! Guess what I did with all my lunch money? I remained his faithful and loyal customer until I left Hong Kong for the States.

When we were moving up north, the moving company would not transport the animals and the fish, so we had to fit them all in our cars. I managed to give two smaller tanks away. I had a small, two-door car then. Imagine putting a large fish tank in the front seat and a tub with all the fish in the trunk. My wife, with the help of her buddy Rebecca, had to transport the cats and the birds. After a five-hour trip, like a miracle, all survived. Goodness, that was only two years ago. It took two semis to move us. One for my wife's pottery and art stuff, and the other our belongings. I never could have imagined that we had so much stuff, especially because we had already gotten rid of half our belongings earlier. I told myself, "This is it, this is your last move, they'll have to carry me out." It amazes me to learn that a lot of folks were born here and have lived here all their lives! How fortunate indeed. I finally found a home for my fish tank – right on top on an antique chest facing the lake. Not to create more shock, yes, fish have feelings too, I tried to arrange the rocks and plants like old days. The water in Milwaukee is fine but what a relief it was to find out that the water condition here is even better.

So, the tank was filled with fresh lake water and the water pump and heater were set. I was told that at nighttime the temperature outside can go under 40F. After the plants were staged and the rocks were placed in a harmonious arrangement – fish love to swim through gaps and cracks between the rocks – I was totally exhausted and went to bed. What an amazing sight it was the next morning when I found out not only had all the fish survived their five-hour trip with no oxygen, they were happily swimming in the new environment. I was thankful and grateful. I grabbed a chair and just sat and watched and watched. They had regained their colors, which meant they were comfortable. What a relief indeed!

I added a few more species to the family. Somehow, they all swim around in groups, greeting each other passing by. No chases, no bites and no bullying each other. My morning ritual is to go to my back porch and listen to the birds while drinking my jasmine tea, then go watch my favorite pet fish. The filter system works so well that the water is crystal clear. The fish appear to be literally gliding on air. Somehow, I wonder if they are observing me, knowing that I am watching them?

Yes, I know my wife loves her cats. After all, we have had them for a long while, but to each their own. I don't have to brush my fish, cleaning up the mess is nothing, there is no foul smell, and my fish don't roam around the kitchen counter and eat the leftovers while knocking the flower vase over with water spilling everywhere. Moreover, when fish food costs less than my beer, what's to complain? I'll keep enjoying my pet fish.

Kids in Luck

A few weeks ago, I was invited to do a cooking demo for the middle school students in Luck. My goodness, there were 60 to 70 eager students there. I made a point to have each
and every one get their hands on in creating their foods. While some were making the Crab Rangoon, I taught the rest how to count in Chinese and told them a little bit about the cuisines of China – that in the South is Cantonese, East is Shanghai, West is Szechuan/Hunan, and North is Beijing. Never thought they would remember a word I said. Yes, it was a bit chaotic with all these energetic kids around, yet they were so well behaved; and everyone was willing to follow instructions. I was most impressed.

Two weeks later, I was in the same classroom, teaching another cooking class. One of my students, Judy Wickland, happened to be one of the teachers that helped out that morning. She smiled at me and told me that she had a surprise for me. Expecting a six-pack of beers, she handed me a folder instead. Inside was a stack of hand drawn thank-you notes and letters thanking me for taking my time to share with them my cooking experience. I read them over and over, and tried not to show any tears. My goodness, how could they be so gracious and thankful for the little that I've done?

Guess I have to share all their thoughts with you, hold your laughs and hold your tears, whatever comes first:

• Dear Peter Kwang, thank you for coming on and teaching us how to make Crab Rangoon. I thought it was so cool that you taught us to say months. – G.E.

• Dear Peter Quan, thank you for teaching us how to cook Crab Rangoon. Peter, you are an interesting guy, I like how you taught us also the Chinese language and the months in Chinese also, 1 – 10. I think you are very generous for giving up your time for us, you are very generous. – M.W.

• Dear Mr. Kwang, thank you for coming and teaching us how to make the food. That was really fun. I liked making the food, I liked that we got to make it all by ourselves. It was really fun, thank you for coming in to teach us how to cook the food. – A.G.

• Dear Mr. Kwang, thank you for teaching me how to make Crab Rangoon. It was really good, and teaching us how to count in Chinese thogh 1 – 10. and the month! Thank you. – J.J.

• Dear Mr. Kwang, thank you so much for coming in and teaching us how to make Crab Rangoon. It has inspired me to learn more about different kinds/types of food. I am planning on, in the future, to make all sorts of foods from Chinese to Asian foods. I really liked the Crab Rangoon and I liked trying new foods. Thank you again for coming in on your own time and cooking for us. – H.P.

• Dear Mr. Kwang, thank you for teaching us how to make Crab Rangoon. It was very good, I will make it again. I also liked when we got to count in Chinese. It was fun, thanks. – B.C.

• Dear Mr. Kwang, I did not get to see you cook that day but I really wish I got to. I did get to see you at Walmart and you seem like a very cool person. I hope we got to see you again. May be I can try your food this time. Sincerely, K.H., or that girl from the Walmart Store

• Dear Mr. Kwong, thank you for making wontons with us. Thanks for taking time out of your day to make my day.

• Dear Mr. Kwang, thank you so much for coming to our school to show us how to make wontons, or in Chinese, won tons. I find Chinese and Japanese fun to write, but that isn't why I'm writing this. I haven't eaten a lot of foreign foods, but this has opened up a whole new world of opportunities. I don't think I've ever met someone that has a first language other than English, which was also awesome to see. You've opened so much of the world to me.

• How's it going, Mr. Kwang. Thank you for coming in and showing us how to make Crab Rangoon. It was very good and one of the best Chinese dishes I have ever had. I am thinking of making it at my house. Thanks again for coming in. – B.E.

• Dear Mr. Kwang, thank you for taking time out of your day to come in to teach us how to make Crab Rangoon. It was my first time ever making and eating crab. I never would have tried it if you never come in. Sincerely, S.A.

• Dear Mr. Kwang, thank you for coming in to teach us to make Crab Rangoon, and how to count to ten in Chinese. For wasting about 3 hours of your life to teach us how to cook and count. – B.L.

• Dear Mr. Kwang, thank you so much for coming to our school and teaching us Chinese and how to make Crab Rangoon. It was delicious. I even made it for dinner that night. – G.E.

• Dear Mr. Kwang, I enjoyed cooking, and getting to make the food ourselves! I learned a lot and it was delicious. Learning to count to ten in Chinese is one of my favorite things I learned that day. I appreciate that you gave up your spare time to teach us to cook Chinese. – E.T.

• Dear Mr. Kwang, thank you for coming into our school and teaching us how to make Crab Rangoon. It was very good and I am thinking about making it soon. Thank you for taking time out of your day to teach us about your culture. I especially enjoyed learning about Chinese numbers and months. Thank you lots. – B.H.

• Dear Mr. Kwong, thank you for teaching us how to make Crab Rangoon. It was tasty. Thank you for teaching us also to count to 10 in Chinese. – C.H.

• Dear Mr. Kwong, I was excited when I found out you were coming and were going to teach us how to make Crab Rangoon. I like trying new foods and it was really good. It was also a lot easier than I thought. I liked learning how to count to ten, even though I don't remember any of them. – K.O.

• Dear Mr. Peter Kwong: I am B.E. and I wanted to thank you for coming in and showing the middle school and I how to make Crab Rangoon. It was really interesting, especially the story you told us while we were waiting for other groups to get done. I won't ever forget this experience. I hope I can make it again sometime, so I can share it with my family and friends. I would like to know your recipe for the sauce though, then I can share that with my family and friends too. We thank you very much for being able to spare some of your time to teach a large middle school class about your experience in China and how to make crab Rangoon, a basic yet delicious dish. I hope to see you perform in your quartet someday. - Sincerely, B.E.

• Dear Mr. Kwong: I am sending you this letter as a token of my appreciation. The day you spent to teach our middle school class how to cook simple Asian cuisine could have been spent doing other things such as staying at home with your family or just sitting around, but you chose to come to our school to help us. The Crab Rangoon recipe you shared with us was amazing and showed us that not all Chinese cuisine is hard to cook. The small lesson you gave to the people that were waiting to cook was interesting considering I have never heard about this topic before. You expanded our knowledge and our skill set. I hope to eventually create this dish for my family and friends along with the sauce. – Sincerely, Z.M.

• Dear Mr. Peter Kwong: my name is A.A., I am a Luck Middle School student. I would like to thank you for coming to our school and showing us how to make Crab Rangoon. It was delicious! The next day my friend Maddy and I made cream cheese wontons using your techniques, they were great. Thank you for giving me a lot of knowledge about Asia and where the flavors and varieties of food came from. Once again thank you for giving up your time, hope to see you soon. – Sincerely, A.A.

• Dear Mr. Kwong: My name is M.B. I am a student at Luck Public Schools. I wanted to thank you for coming to our school during the Asia project to teach us how to make Crab Rangoon. It was so delicious and easy to make. My friend Audrie A. and I made cream cheese wontons on our own using what you taught us, and they were amazing. We had many people try them and they all loved them. I also enjoyed you telling us about all other foods "sections" in Asia. Your enthusiasm in what you do is so inspiring and it shows me to do what makes you happy.

Thank you again for visiting our school to teach us how to make Crab Rangoon and I hope you come to visit again sometime. - Sincerely, M.B.

• Dear Peter Kwong Thank you for coming in to our school

and teaching us how to make Crab Rangoon. It was super good. I can't believe how easy it is to make, and how fast you can make it is awesome. I liked how you talked about how you were a chef, and about your personal life. - Sincerely, T.Z.

• Dear Mr. Kwong, I am very thankful for you coming to our school to show us all how to make Crab Rangoon. It was very good and I enjoyed learning how to make it. I thought it was easy and fun. I also really liked the sauce that you made with it, that was really good. I am going to try and make Crab Rangoon at my house sometime for my family. I think they would like it too. Thank you for teaching us about the different Chinese foods. Thank you for talking to us about what your life was like growing up in Hong Kong. - Sincerely, A.K.

• Dear Peter Kwong, I am writing you a thank-you letter to thank you for coming to our school and teaching us how to make Crab Rangoon. I personally would've liked it better if there wasn't any crab because I'm not a huge fan of seafood, but you couldn't really taste the crab. The sauce you made for us for really good too. I'm glad you didn't make it spicy because I don't like spicy things at all. Thank you for taking the time out of your day to come and teach 2-3 different groups how to make Crab Rangoon and letting us try and make a few ourselves. Thank you for telling us about where different Chinese foods come from and how to remember them. It was nice that you talked while other groups were waiting for their turn and for the food to be done, so no one would get bored. Thank you for talking about where you're from, where you live now, what you do for a living, and about Chinese food. - Sincerely, K.M.

• Dear Mr. Kwong, thank you for teaching us how to make Crab Rangoon. It was much easier than I thought it might be but you already had the Cream Cheese and Crab mix already. It was a new kind of taste because I don't eat Chinese food. But it was good. Thank you again for teaching part of your culture to us and for coming to our school. - Sincerely, W.J.

• Dear Mr. Kwong you taught me a really easy way to make a really good food. I tried different options like pork, cheese, beef, and there are still so many options to try. I am grateful for all you have taught me. Now that I know how to make Crab Rangoon I can teach my parents how. - Sincerely, N.S.

• Dear Mr. Kwong, thank you for teaching us about Asian cooking. It was fun watching and learning about food from Asia. - Sincerely, C.G

• Dear Mr. Kwang, thank you for taking time out of your day to teach us how to make Crab Rangoon. – B.O.

• Dear Mr. Kwang, I appreciate you coming in to our school and spending your time with us. I thought the food was so good I had to make them for my family. I appreciate you showing us your cooking skills. – G.J.

What a precious experience. Hope these letters and kind words touch your heart as much as they have touched mine.

The difference between a chef and a cook

A lot of folks have asked me what the difference between a chef and a cook is. Goodness, such a tough question. It is like asking the question of, "Do you fish?" And "Do you know how to fish?" Anyone can fish, including me. Get a pole, a box filled with different kinds of hooks and sinkers and a tub of fresh worms. Off I go "fishing." But most of the time, some panfish and largemouth bass would be my pride and joy. However, when I read that 2- to 3-lb. walleyes, and 30" to 40" northern pikes were caught, and some even by 10- to 12-year- olds, I can't help but wonder, just what did I do wrong? As my good friend Geezer Bob would tell me, "Anyone can fish, but it takes something special to be a fisherman." What wisdom indeed. Hence, I am sharing his words of wisdom about cooking,

"Anyone can pick up cooking, but it takes someone special in becoming a chef."

I used to teach at a culinary school in Milwaukee, and it was rewarding to see the graduates get nabbed by different food institutions including hotels, country clubs and five-star restaurants, before they even graduated. But it was a tough journey going through four years of drilling and grilling, learning and knowing everything about food and the business. A lot of folks believe that just by opening a restaurant, folks will pour in and the cash register will be "ka-chinging" all the time with money pouring in. How I wish that life could be that easy and simple. When I was a restaurant consultant, I had a retired couple call me for help. They had a nice pension after retirement and wanted to buy a restaurant to run it profitably and keep the rest of their retirement life comfortable. Unfortunately, it didn't work that way. I don't want to go into details, but they ended up selling the restaurant at a loss. There was nothing that I could do to help, as they were too deep in debt. A sad story indeed, but the truth.

Most students were fascinated by the TV shows with all of the celebrity chefs, making millions of dollars just by cooking and looking cool. But in becoming a celebrity chef, there are so many factors involved. Timing is one of them – to be in the right place at the right time. So, what makes a good cook? To be able to follow orders and recipes, be able to work well with others, to have common sense and to have a passion for foods and people. To do the same thing over and over every day can be challenging.

When I was a prep cook, at the end of the day, even though I was exhausted, I was happy knowing that what I did contributed to making someone happy.

So, what does it take to become a good cook?

Know all the basic skills:

• Knife skills including mincing, dicing, slicing, julienne and quartering.

• Cooking methods including braise, fry, steam, bake, grill, saute and stir-fry.

• Portion and styling; how each plate should look and be arranged consistently.

• Following recipes so that all foods are cooked the same way and taste the same each time.

Understand general restaurant procedures:

• Opening and closing procedures - follow the guidelines to make sure that all of the equipment is cleaned and sanitized for the next shift and all foods are stored promptly afterward.

• Food serving temperatures – serve cold food under 40F, and hot food above 140F. Anything in between can make people sick and is called the danger zone.

• Understanding all sanitation standards such as cross contamination, hand washing and food stored 6″ above the floor.

So, what makes a chef a chef?

• Master all the basic skills – with a sharp knife, one should be able to slice, dice and mince blindfolded.

• Know how to set up a proper kitchen – it is like playing drums. How do you set up your drum set so you can go "boom boom, ding ding, and dang dang" at the same spot?

• Know the equipment needed. Depending on the concept, what equipment does one need to perform all the functions

– a fryer, a grill, a stove with burners? Each concept requires different equipment.

• Have the ability to teach and train – rather than barking orders, does the chef have the patience to work with his subordinates so they all know what the expectations are, and understanding the big picture?

• Possess creativity – does the chef have intuition to create entrees that are unique and different; and that would please the senses – smell, appearance and flavor? Anyone can make Chicken Cacciatore, but what make yours different? A chef always thinks outside the box, by utilizing what the market has to offer. A cook would follow recipes, but a chef creates them with what he/she has on hand. To take an ordinary ingredient and makes it a specialty, like cow's cheek, would take a lot of creativity.

• Understanding timing – how to orchestrate different events to be executed at the same time. Imagine serving eight weddings on a Saturday evening. Each wedding varies from 100 to 500 guests, all with different entrees, and each group would love to be served at the same time, 6 p.m. sharp. Possible? Absolutely.

• Understanding profit – we are here to make a profit. No business can sustain on a negative cash flow. Understanding the profit and loss statement, the plate costs, the profit margin and the operation standards would help.

I love to watch the reruns of Julia Child's cooking show. Wouldn't you like to know the story of a lady who never cooked in her life and how she became a legend in foods after her first career ended? And with Jacques Pepin, they were my inspirations for years to come. "What separates a good chef from a great chef?" someone once asked Jacques Pepin. He responded, "To be a good chef you have to be a good technician. To be a great chef you not only have to be a good technician, but you also have to have talent, and you have to have love." Yes, he also taught us that food doesn't make sense unless you share it with someone.

To be a cook, or to become a chef, it really doesn't matter, as long as you do it with love and share with others. After all, isn't that what life is all about?

Outdoor survival

My wife got me this little "Pocket Guide to Outdoor Survival" by Ron Cordes and Stan Bradshaw. Wish I had this earlier, so I would be more prepared for living in the North Woods. It is a different lifestyle altogether. Being a city boy all my life, there were streetlights everywhere I went, and wild animals could only be seen at the zoo. And here, I see flocks of wild turkey roaming through our backyard; and I almost ran into deer and raccoons a few times. Where are they from? Just jumping out of the woods playing the game "Dare you to hit me"?

I was driving to Iowa to attend my niece's graduation a few months ago. A long drive indeed – five hours each way, ugh. Yes, I am learning, you have to prepare to drive an hour or more to places if you live here in the North Woods. Had to drink a lot of tea to keep me awake. On my way home back to St. Croix Falls, while driving nonchalantly, listening to my classical station, I heard a "boom" all of a sudden; and then I noticed that my windshield was totally shattered, even the rearview mirror had fallen off. Not knowing what actually happened, I kept driving for another good half a mile. Then all of a sudden, it dawned on me, "Oh my Lord, I've been hit by some UFO."

I pulled the car over, turned my emergency blinkers on, and stepped out of the car, trying to investigate just what had happened. The feathers that were stuck on the windshield indicated it must have been a bird, a really huge bird indeed. Kind folks stopped by and asked me if I needed any help. I had no idea what to do except to call 911.

Fortunately enough, there was a patrolman closed by, and he was there in less than 10 minutes. He examined the windshield and exclaimed that I was indeed hit by a low-flying wild turkey. A turkey? The one we gathered around at Thanksgiving table? What was it doing flying around and hitting my windshield? Then the officer told me that it must have been a bird that weighed 50 pounds or more, judging on the impact (so, it could have fed a party or 25 or more). The whole windshield did cave in, and thank goodness, it didn't break, or I would have been a goner. So, after paying $3,000 of repair damage, I am on my way to becoming a country boy.

All that reminded me of my first encounter with Mother Nature. And how I wish I had the pocketbook then. We live on a small lake near St. Croix Falls and bought a canoe right after we moved in. Darryl, my brother-in-law, helped us build a dock that could harbor the canoe on the lakeshore. I have to tell this story. Darryl was with the Army for years. We first met when he just returned from a deployment from Afghanistan. Of course we invited him to join our Sunday family dinner. I don't remember what I made that evening, may be some beef stew? Anyway, he took one bite and then he looked me straight in the eye, and said, "Peter, will you marry me?"

Our whole family (including his future wife), laughed. But knowing that he had been eating the Army packaged meals for years, anything would taste good. But he liked my beef stew. A great relationship had begun.

Anyway, Darryl was an engineer in the Army, and his job was to "make things work." If a tank or jeep got blown up, how to make them work again? Or, better yet, how to get rid of them before the enemy got their hands on them? Not having any experience in building a dock or pier, he created one for us. His family came over one day, and he got piles of wood planks from Menards and was busy sawing and hammering away. By using a couple of pickle barrels as floaters, Darryl built a floating dock that could harbor the canoe, all in a day's work. It was so easy to get in and out of the canoe with the dock that he built. My wife and I went out a few times, and that was so pleasant. But that's when trouble begins.

One early evening, while my wife was still at work, I thought I could just go out and have a canoe ride on my own. Or better yet, may be a little fishing; and have some fresh pan- fried lake fish to surprise her when she got home. The wind sock on the dock was waving fiercely and even the lake was having white caps. But I thought to myself, This is a small lake, and the deepest end is only 8' deep, what can it do to me?

And off I paddled, with two of my fishing poles and a can

of fresh-dug worms from our garden. It was easy to paddle out, as the current was just carrying me. I settled my two fishing poles on the slot at the edge of the canoe and was just thinking that a good time had just begun. Then a "whoosh," one of my fishing poles was blown into the water. I thought it was a bad omen and was trying to paddle back to my dock, but the canoe would not move. The undercurrent was so strong that no matter how hard I paddled, the canoe wouldn't budge.

And the worst part, it was getting dark, and I could barely see my dock. I saw my landmark – the two tall pine trees next to the dock, and was paddling there with all my might. However, the canoe refused to go where I wanted. I had to back paddle to move forward. Talk about confusing. And finally, I was carried to the edge of some point that looked like my landmark. But no, it wasn't. At least I was smart enough to pull the canoe off the water and try to walk to dry land. But then it got dark, really fast.

While I managed to push the canoe into the tall weeds (or whatever they call it), I was stuck on my end. I couldn't move forward as the path was blocked by bushes with thorns. And I was stepping in muck that would suck me in every time I made a move. "Why this, Lord?" I told myself, "I thought North Woods is going to be fun." And it was totally dark. I couldn't see my fingers in front of my face. Fear sank in, finally. "Am I going to spend the night here, feeding the northern pikes?" I thought to myself. I have heard about their sharp teeth. Wouldn't dare to move an inch, I held on for what seemed like hours. Cold, bleeding and filled with fear; oh, what fun living in the North Woods. A thousand questions of why, why, why ran through my mind.

Then out from nowhere, a tiny light came from a distance. And that was my wife with her flashlight, searching for me.

If that was not true love. Or maybe she was looking for me to make her dinner? Anyway, she heard me and saved me. Hence, I carry her "Pocket Guide to Outdoor Survival" every place I go now. Survival 101, and respect Mother Nature.

Career Day

Irecently was invited to speak to the students at Osceola High School on their Career Day. They have more than 500 students in the school, made me feel young again to be around all these energetic teenagers. How many years ago when I was at their age? I was amazed to find that there were 30 or more speakers who were willing to talk to the students about their career paths. Many of those speakers are alumni. It just amazes me that living up here in the North Woods, folks are from here, and they remain living here their whole lives. For whatever reasons, whether they moved away to live or work in other states or countries, they always find their way back home. Roots are deep here. If not for my granddaughter, the move up here would never have happened, and the new roots would not have started.

I did much volunteer work while living in Milwaukee, with Junior Achievement, SCORE, which is the Service Corps of Retired Executives, and the HCCW (Hispanic Chamber of Commerce Wisconsin). How a Chinese guy got involved with the Hispanic Chamber of Commerce is another story, as I don't even speak Spanish. My Spanish is limited to:
- Hola – How are you?
- Muy bien – very good
- Dame una cervesa, por favor. – Give me another beer, please.
- Donde esta el bano – Where is the bathroom?

Somehow, I got by with those four phrases every place I went in the Hispanic communities. Even survived living in Guatemala working as a consultant. But that was a long, long time ago. It was a different world then. There would be a guard carrying a shotgun in all shops and restaurants, especially in front of a bank. Did I feel safe? Perhaps. One morning, I heard firecrackers going off early in the morning. When I asked the concierge what they were celebrating, he answered, "No senor; that was machine guns going off." I left that afternoon, and never returned.

To tell the story of my career was a trip, just where to begin? To walk down memory lane once again after all these years, with all those young, wondering eyes staring at me, it was some experience indeed. So I told them about coming from Hong Kong. They were amazed at the story of how Hong Kong became a British colony a hundred years ago. I don't mind repeating it again, as it is some great story.

At the end of the 18th century, China was so corrupted and weak (the empress used the money for defense to build a summer palace instead) that all the countries around the world wanted to have a piece of this juicy meat. Britain, at that time, was using Hong Kong to import opium from India to China. There were opium dens everywhere, and all the youngsters were getting "stoned" instead of being productive. The governor of Hong Kong finally had enough, and decided to gather all the opium, and burnt it all in downtown Hong Kong. It must have been one heck of a party, with everyone nearby inhaling the fumes. Needless to say, the British were ticked, as their fortune went up in smoke, literally. So, in protest, they sent an army to fight the Chinese soldiers. Guess who lost? The mighty Chinese lost to an army which was one-thousandth the size. Unlike the Japanese, who demanded zillions in gold and silver, which they used later to build up an army to start WWII; the British just asked for Hong Kong, to be ceded to them for 99 years. So, for 99 years, Hong Kong belonged to the British Empire, and was governed by their rules. Can you imagine if the Columbian drug lords, who sold drugs to our kids, won a war against the U.S., and wanted to take Wisconsin for 99 years to be governed by their rules? Ridiculous as it seems, that was the truth with the ceding of Hong Kong.

I told the story many times about my journey to the States, and how and why I chose the U.S. to become my destination for further education. While growing up, we had banquets for distant relatives who had immigrated to the States earlier. Just to show off that they had "made" it upon their visit back to Hong Kong, they would hand me a crispy $5 bill as "lucky money" when we met. Twenty-five cents a month was my allowance, and this stranger was handing me a $5 bill. What to believe? Yes, America was the place to be, where everything must be paved in gold. Little did I know, until later, the truth about all these relatives - they worked in sweat shops, living in tight quarters with many others for years, then saved up enough money and returned home just to show others that they made it. I was fooled.

Since it was Career Day, I asked the students what was the difference between a career and a job? One of the students answered, "A job is something that you have to do to earn a living; make money working so you can pay bills. A career is something that you enjoy doing; you can utilize your passion and have fun just working." Wow, so nice to hear that from a 15-year-old. A career is something that you enjoy doing, fulfilling your dreams, and devoted to helping others in the process. I was deeply touched.

I got into the hospitality field starting as a dishwasher, and then moved up through the ranks to become prep cook, line cook, then a waiter, bartender, and finally became a manager, supervisor, and director of operations and whatever. It was a long journey indeed, but I enjoyed every step. Students mentioned what they wanted to be – a doctor, an artist, an engineer, a zookeeper, a designer ... I looked at them with admiration. At their age, I had no idea what my career would be. Somehow, I shared with them my two bits of wisdom – "Happiness is not about making a lot of money. You'll find true happiness if you:
- Know what you are doing,
- Believe in what you are doing, and
- Love what you're doing.
Wish them all the best in choosing their paths.

The Indianhead Chorus in concert

The Indianhead Chorus concert

Our Indianhead Barbershop Chorus had a show a few weeks ago, and for those who missed it, make sure you make plans to attend next year. We had two shows at the Amery High School, at 2 p.m. and 7 p.m., and both were almost sold out. Being a new member of the chorus, I was amazed and impressed.

Yes, singing barbershop is a hobby, but what a hobby indeed. Where else can you meet a bunch of guys who love to sing and devote their time to creating harmony together with each other? There are four parts in the chorus: lead, bass, tenor and baritone. The lead part is easy, just carry the tune. The bass singers have a natural deep voice and the tenor carries a higher note. The baritone sings the part that doesn't make any sense by itself, yet, when combined with the other three voices, creates a tone that rings. I admire the baritone brothers as they are always the butts of all jokes (that they can't carry a tune). Yet, without them, it will be like an item short of your combo package. Can you imagine eating a Big Mac without fries? Well, something like that.

I first joined the SPEBSQSA almost 20 years ago while living in Atlanta, Ga. What in the world does SPEBSQSA stands for, you might ask. Well, are you ready? It stands for Society for the Preservation and Encouragement of Barbershop Quartets Singing in America. I joined a group called the Big Chicken Chorus, which was named after the KFC symbol on Main Street or Peachtree Street; yes, a big huge head of a chicken that stood 40' tall. Very few folks who live in Atlanta actually are from Atlanta. We lived in a cul-de-sac that housed about 12 families, and only two families were from Georgia, all other families came from somewhere else: Kansas, Kentucky, South Carolina, Wisconsin (Yes! do you believe it?) and Illinois. There were all these big corporations – IBM, Coca- Cola and hundreds of Fortune 500 companies - that chose Atlanta to be their headquarters. New recruits come and go all the time. Anyway, one of the neighbors came over one day, and invited me to their guest night. He belonged to the Big Chicken Chorus, and they were looking for new comers. I don't read music but I love to sing. He assured me that you do not need to read music in order to sing with the group. There are learning tapes that you can listen to. And after you follow those songs a few times, you can easily tag along. So, I took a chance and I went for the evening. I'm so glad I did, I was hooked and joined them immediately.

I was always mesmerized by barbershop singing. Growing up in Hong Kong, I first encountered barbershop singing while watching a short film promoting the opening of Disneyland in California. I wasn't attracted much to the Pirates of the Caribbean or the Matterhorn rides then. But my eyes glued to the screen when they showed a barbershop quartet singing on Main Street. I didn't know anything about the four-part harmony then but the sound just intrigued me. I knew they all sounded different, but I couldn't figure out how it could be possible that such harmony could come together. Then, actually singing with the chorus solved the mystery that harbored in me all these years.

Before one can officially become a member of the chorus, one has to learn the "polecat" songs which are sung throughout the whole society. Whether you are initiated in Australia, the States, England or Iceland, you have to know all those songs first. I once was in Toronto, attending a wedding between my buddy's daughter and a British gentleman. I met the groom's family and was heartily chatting with the groom's father with my long-lost British accent and the topic of barbershop singing came up. His face lightened up when

I told him that I sing lead with my chorus. He told me that he sang bass with his. Naturally, I asked him if he knew any polecat songs. Of course he did. So, we decided to entertain our guests with a few songs. Without any rehearsals, two strangers performed flawlessly, singing those songs enthusiastically. The crowd went wild. That, my dear friends, is the magic of barbershop singing – we have friends all over the world.

If you can't read music (like me), it is fine. I did it, and so can you. Like cooking, singing is from the heart. I love it when my guests finish every morsel on their plates, and same with watching the guests absorbing the harmony and message of each song that we are projecting. We are telling stories – being in love, out of love, of joy and happiness, and of sadness and loneliness.

Our chorus also does church sing-outs on some Sunday mornings. And look for us around Valentine season, we have quartets going around the community singing love songs to your loved one with roses. And talk about brownie points! A good portion of the money that we raise each year is donated to Interfaith Caregivers of Polk and Burnett counties.

Winter Wonderland

Without any proper warning, winter finally arrives. Overnight, the temperature droppped to two digits below zero. Just a few weeks ago I was bragging how good it felt basking in the 60-degree weather. Brrrr! We have bird feeders around our yards, as my wife is an enthusiastic bird-watcher. We had golden finches and hummingbirds zipping around in summertime, but in the cold weather, there are downy woodpeckers, blue jays, juncos, chickadees, cardinals, nuthatches and many more. My office window faces the lake and I get to watch all the different birds munching on the seeds hanging on the feeders. Every two or three days, I have to refill the feeders with more seeds and suet. For some reason, all birds love the suet. It is kind of expensive, so to speak (yes, cost more than my beer). But it is our entertainment and it is cheaper than going to a theater.

I've learned to like animals as my wife is an animal lover.

I still can't cook roast duck, rack of lamb or venison in the house. Heaven forbid, having Bambi in the oven. We have two cats, down from three, three birds, down from seven, and 15, plus or minus a few, tropical fish in our home. A happy family indeed.

It snowed 4 to 6 inches last night and more this evening, with temperatures dropping to minus 25 F. Looking out the window, the lake is already frozen solid. I've even seen crazy folks trying to do some ice fishing right outside our dock. Are they in their right mind? What if they fall in when the ice cracks? "But look at all these beautiful fish that I caught," they would exclaim. How can I argue with that? Happiness is not defined by how much money you've got but how many fish you caught. Didn't Confucius say that?

Anyway, we had problems with all the squirrels invading our bird feeders. No matter what I do to block their feeding habits, they've outsmarted me. I put on a "squirrel-proof" feeder, just to find them hanging upside down, feeding on it with a smile. They make that giggling and laughing sound that drives me nuts. I was even thinking of getting a squirrel gun and shooting them. Or hire Geezer Bob's grandson, he could shoot them with bow and arrows. What a guy.

After many tries, I finally invested in a dome that goes inside the pole where you hang the feeder. My sweet revenge. I saw the little squirrel jumping to the feeder, just to hit the dome and fall off of the rail. After a few more tries of jumping up, getting blocked and falling off, he finally subsided. I guess I don't know how that makes me feel – at least I'm smarter than a squirrel.

I'd never seen snow until I came to the States. It was the most sensational feeling to walk on a snow patch, to touch and feel the snowflakes, and hear the squishing sound beneath my feet. Now that the snow is accumulating, the old senses have lingered, how beautiful and how wonderful it feels. We have the tallest pine tree on our lake. Eagles rest on the higher branches and even the wild turkeys perch on the lower twigs, squawking for their companions to join them.

For whatever the reason, the snow never blocks the moon from shining through. I often wake up at 3 or 4 a.m., just to notice that our front yard is glowing with a pure white light, so soft and smooth. I would walk out in the porch in my pajamas and feel the presence of winter. Cold, yes. Peaceful, yes. Serenity, yes, yes, yes. Standing there and staring at the sky, I forget about the cold. I enjoy just feeling the feeling of being there with nature and with the environment. There is a certain calm and peace that one doesn't sense living in a cement forest with colorful streetlights, the noise of passing automobiles and the distant trains passing by or the landing of another aircraft in the wee hours.

As if by magic, the bird feeder is like a main terminal for all birds. Without any directions, all birds would follow their feeding orders and wait for their turns. While a certain species may go full-force to get their shares, other birds hang on the branches nearby, patiently waiting for their turns. Once in in great while, two or three birds argue for their seniorities, as to who should be first to feed. But the matter would soon settle as there are plenty of slots indeed, for all to enjoy a feast.

On a cold evening, couldn't help but think about this warm coffee drink. It was one of my most popular drinks in my bartending days, so here it is, enjoy.

Keoki coffee

Fill up a cup with 4 oz. of coffee or hot chocolate. Add 1 oz. brandy and 1/2 oz. of kahlua or your preferred coffee liqueur.

Add a dab of whipped cream on top and there you have it. Merry Amery nip - I made up that name.

Fill a cup with 4 oz. of coffee or hot chocolate. Add 1 oz. of brandy and 1/2 oz. of menthe/schnapps. Add a dab of whipped cream on top.

I can't believe how fast 2016 has come and gone. I hope 2017 will be a joyous and prosperous year for all.

More on Chinese Dinner

After the banquet with The Roost at Spooner Golf Club on Chinese New Year Day, we hosted our own dinner at our home to welcome the New Year. It is a tradition to have families and friends together with "lucky" foods, which are supposed to bring fortune, prosperity and health. No, we didn't have the traditional firecrackers crackling and dragon dance boogieing on the front yard, but we made it up with food. Our good friends Irene and Robin were invited to join our feast. They are also in Carolyn Wedin's writing class with me. At the dinner table, Irene sat next to me and was commenting on each dish. A light turned on then. "Irene," I started, "why don't you write something about your dining experience? I write about foods all the time but it is from a chef's standpoint. From you, who loves foods and loves to write, I think the readers would have a different perspective. What do you think?" I have said that many times before but this time I was serious. What better way to hear about a dish than from another food lover? While most of my students would describe my dishes with, "delicious," "wonderful," "wow" or "that's the best I've ever had." Yet when I asked, "So what do you really like about it?" all they did was smile.

After much pleading and begging, she finally agreed and here is her version. Many thanks to Irene for taking the time from her busy schedule to compose this. I hope you all enjoy it as much as I do. Thank you, Irene, my dear friend.

Celebrating the New Year
by Irene Bugge

I picked up the bulging purse (pot sticker) with my chopsticks and bit off the tip of the pork and vegetable wonton-wrapped delicacy. After drizzling spicy dipping sauce into the opened pouch, I ate the rest in two bites. I could not resist devouring another.

And so began our celebration of Lunar or Chinese New Year on Jan. 29. This was the second time during the month of January that chef Peter Kwong, St. Croix Valley's own celebrity chef, had invited my husband and me to a 2017 New

Year's Day dinner party.

The first gathering, as you might guess, was on Jan. 1, pot stickers were the appetizer at that party, too. The duplication was intentional because pot stickers are the quintessential Chinese symbol for prosperity. Other-

Pot Stickers with dipping sauce

wise the two New Year's celebratory meals were completely different.

Chef Peter served Mongolian firepot on Jan. 1. When we arrived, two woks filled with boiling broth, made in advance from beef, pork and chicken bones, were bubbling away in the middle of the dining room table. The savory aroma greeted us as soon as we entered the Kwongs cozy log home. Peter had also cut raw meats, seafood, tofu and vegetables into bite-sized pieces, ready to be cooked. But we learned that Peter was not doing the cooking – his guests were.

Lotus Blossoms

When we took our places at the table, we each found two small shallow dishes, in addition to our plate, chopsticks, wineglass and teacup. A wire basket attached to a long handle rested in one dish. The other was filled with Peter's 2soy-based dipping sauce. In addition, a huge bowl of steaming rice sat on the table along with a pot of jasmine tea.

We were instructed to put shrimp balls into our wire baskets and carefully place the baskets into the boiling broth, hooking the handles on the edge of the wok. When our food was

Triple exotic mushrooms Cantonese

cooked through we pulled our baskets out of the rich, hot liquid and ate our fill of shrimp balls dipped in spicy sauce with rice.

The process continued – fill basket, plunge into boiling broth, remove when cooked, dip in sauce, eat, repeat, for sliced pork, chicken, tofu, lobster, salmon and finally vegetables. Each addition enhanced the flavor of the already robust broth and culminated in the final course, the grand finale of the meal, a bowl of liquid umami with noodles. An unforget-

Salmon with ginger garlic sauce

table meal.

Imagine our surprise three weeks later, when we were invited to celebrate New Year's Day at the home of the Kwongs again – this time Chinese New Year's. Peter's wife, Colleen, told us that he planned to serve a multicourse feast. We thought that the Mongolian firepot had been a feast. We could only speculate about what he would prepare for the most important Chinese celebration of the year - Thanksgiving, Christmas and New Year's rolled into one.

Crispy chow mein with vegetables

Starters, as you already know, included pot stickers followed by san choy or lotus blossom (lettuce wraps made with pork and sprinkled with peanuts). Lotus blossom rhymes with "obtaining fortune" in Chinese, building on the theme of prosperity.

Next, Peter prepared an abalone and shitake mushroom stir-fry with tofu. I had never eaten abalone mushrooms before. They taste like their name and are delicious. In addition, these meaty mushrooms are believed to foster growth and prosperity.

Shrimp with snow peas

Platters of piping hot salmon cooked with ginger and scallion arrived next. Yu (fish) rhymes with the Chinese word for leftovers. Leftover food after a meal signifies that you had enough to eat, another sign of prosperity.

After we had our fill of salmon, crispy

noodles with Cantonese stir-fried vegetables were served. The egg noodles were first boiled and then panfried before being topped with vegetables. In China, noodles are a symbol of longevity – the longer the noodle the better.

The last dish on the menu was shrimp and snow peas. The Chinese word for shrimp rhymes with "ha." "Ha," in both Chinese and English, is laughter. So the meal ended with joy, although there had been much laughter around the table while we ate course after course, and for all who attended, stomachs bulging like purses.

As Chef Kwong would say: Kung hei fat choi – Happy (Chinese) New Year!

Pesky Squirrels

We used to have a squirrel feeder in Milwaukee. It was a large gallon glass jar that hooked up to an opening that you could nail to a tree. You could take the jar out, and filled it with whatever food you want, and then put it back in the feeder, and then just watched the show. Think about it, the openings of the feeder are the same size of the mouth of the jar (about 2" wide), just how in the world those squirrels could get the food out of that tiny opening? It would take me a while to shuffle a 12" flour tortilla through the tiny mouth of the jar. Somehow, those little rascals could pull the prize a little bit at a time, and managed to place the piece in a perfect angle before he made the final move. It seemed effortless, but it worked. I would be using brute force the whole time. I learned a lot about being patient and use my brain instead of just using my muscles. Then I got creative, putting ears of corn in the jar and tried to watch how they managed to get those long husk out of the tiny openings. I think they knew I was watching, and nobody showed up. The next morning, all the corn were gone. Wish I had an auto video to see just how they did it. What clever rascals.

Living in the North Woods, a different story unfolded, these cute rascals are not as cute anymore. My wife is a bird watcher, and she has bird feeders everywhere, and have seeds for the finches, seeds for the blue jays & cardinals, suet for the woodpeckers, and nectar for the humming birds. Somehow, those feeders have become squirrel haven. I don't mind them sharing the foods, but they would cling on to the feeders and devoured the whole content. Meanwhile, all other birds would fly around the feeders, waiting for their turns, which hardly came by, as the feeders would be empty after the squirrels left. Tired of their greed, I thought of different methods to keep those pesky squirrels away from the feeders. I spent a fortune getting longer poles to hang the feeders, thinking that they would be out of reach for any normal size animals. However, every time I turned around, a furry rodent would be hanging upside down on the feeder having a field day.

Squirrels are smart animals, and I've watched videos of squirrels running through an obstacle course designed to train the young marines (in a much smaller scale, of course). These rodents have to climb up a rope to a platform, then hang on to a tight rope to reach the far end hundreds of feet away. Then climb up and down a brick wall hanging on to another rope; I forgot about the rest, too complicated. To the Marines, that's intensive physical training. Yet to the squirrels, the reward is just a handful of nuts. To go through all that for a handful of nuts, are they nuts?

Finally, I got two different sets of dome shaped "squirrel proof" protectors. But I've to use the knowledge I acquired in high school in order to make good use of it. Squirrels never attended school, just how they figured all these angles and tactics? If I apply the dome too low on the pole, the pest will just jump and grab on to the edge of the dome. After an 180 degree swing, he would move on to the feeder and have a nice Smorgasbord. So I finally moved the dome up higher, kind of in between the ground and the feeder. Knowing that even those pesky rodents have sharp claws, they couldn't possibly grab on to the edge of the dome and have the chance to do his 180 degree somersault. It worked. However, a few weeks later, a hungry bear out of hibernation would bend the pole to the ground, smashed the suet container, split the feeder in half, and ate all the contents. So, that's what living in the North Woods is all about. At least the bear didn't come inside the house, our cupboard is always loaded with food!

Living in big cities my whole life, with street lights in every street corner; it was really scary my first few weeks living in the country side. I got lost even with the GPS on.

Imagine driving on a county road, with no lights and no road signs. I remember that one night after teaching at River Falls, I was driving home after a terrible storm. Thank goodness, the pouring rain stopped. Yet, the fog started to build up. The road was like a movie from 'Frankenstein', I could barely see the foggy road, while shadows of the haunting trees would be winding all over, and the howling from the distant coyotes seemed like they were only 5' away. Worse, part of the road on Hwy 65 was closed and blocked off. I took a detour just to find out after half an hour drive, I was back in the same spot; where is mother when I needed her?

I've finally out smarted the squirrels in the front yard, by moving the dome at an angle that is impossible for any squirrels to reach. Good Lord, four years of college education just to figure that out? But then the battle at the back yard remains. That's the place where we have our humming bird nectar, our thistle for the finches, and the suet and seeds for other birds. Somehow, the squirrels find ways to reach them all. So, I put a dome to one of the feeders, thinking that it would be safe. After a few more times of adjusting the angle of how the pole should hang out, I've finally succeeded. It was trial and error to adjust the dome, and watching different squirrels trying to jump up, and hit the dome first before they fell off to the ground 15' below. It was most entertaining. He did it a few times, and finally gave up. Triumph came over me, what sweet revenge indeed! But did I really win the battle?? Somehow, I was astonished finding that I a big fat gray squirrel was hanging upside down, feasting on the seeds meant to be for the finches. He jumped from the branches above instead! Attack from air if ground assault doesn't work; what tactics! No domes can ever protect my feeders. What to do? What to do? May be I've to hire Geezer Bob's grandson and guard the feeders with his bows and arrows.

Tipping in restaurants

A while back, I read an article from a mom whose daughter got a lousy tip from a group of customers who were demanding, yet left her absolutely nothing for her service. Needless to say, she was devastated. That was rude, disrespectful and absolutely unethical. And I would be more than just "devastated." (Sorry, can't use words that are unprintable). But who's to blame? And what to do?

Most restaurants in the European countries discourage tipping. But a service charge of 10 to 15 percent is already included in the bill. In New York City, a few restaurants have already started a new trend and discourage tipping also. They are paying the servers a higher wage, but increase the menu prices accordingly. The industry is already competitive the way it is; can the restaurants survive if they keep increasing their prices?

Well, while the big chains are benefiting from lower food costs because they purchase in bulk, the rest of the family restaurants simply can't compete. Most restaurants operate on a one-third system – one-third of the revenue pays for food, 1/3 pays for labor, and the other 1/3 pays for the overhead; and whatever leftover is profit. (Yes, one-third plus one- third plus one-third equals one. So, what's left for profit? An interesting question indeed.)

Yes, the hospitality industry is a tough one. According to the National Restaurant Association, there are over 1 million restaurants in the U.S., and 7 out of 10 are family operations. Over 14.4 million are employed in the industry, and the minimum wage is around $7.25 an hour. Some might receive a higher wage as cooks or bartenders. However, the servers receive an average of only $2.13 an hour, just because they are "tipped employees." The IRS doesn't care if you do not get tipped; however, if you ever do, they will want their share right away. So, the $5.12 difference comes from the "tips." And if the servers do not get "tipped," they are out of luck and pretty much working for free. Now we all understand why our young lady server was so upset. She spent all night working hard for "nothing!" What if it was you, or someone close to you? How would that make you feel?

My college tuition came from the tips working in a restaurant. And while most guests left me a 15- to 20-percent gratuity, I did have my fair share of nontippers. But then again, what to do? After I realized that the tips come from the percentage of their bills, I switched my focus and tried my best to increase their bills' total. I was practicing the skills of "upselling" or "suggestive selling" without knowing it.

TIPS means "to insure proper service.' So, what is proper service? It is the total experience of expectations from a guest's standpoint. Most guests are willing to pay more if they have a memorable dining experience, with an opportunity to try something unique and special. There are no written rules on tipping, but, after working in the industry all these years, most institutions agree on these guidelines:

• 5 to 10 percent - for someone who just takes your order, serves your food, and brings you the check. The server does not know what's on the menu and what the "specials" are. Their response is always, "Everything on the menu is good," or "Don't know, never tried it. Let me ask the cook." You have to ask for more water, napkins and ketchup with your fries, or whatever. But you can see him/her chatting at the side station. Or worse, hear the whole conversation.

• 10 to 15 percent - does more than taking the order and bringing you the plates. They know what you need without you asking, and give you enough privacy with your dining mate. However, like a miracle, they will show up from nowhere to take care of your needs. Even say, "Thank you, and come see us again," when presenting the check.

• 15 to 25 percent - provide a total dining experience with friendly suggestions and not being pushy:

• "Have you folks tried our crab cakes before? That's my most favorite appetizer."

• "Our chef has prepared these specials for this evening. And this _____ is just unbelievable!"

• "May I suggest pinot noir with your entree? It is light and elegant. You can also have it by the glass if you prefer."

• "Enjoy your dinner. And don't forget to save some room for our special dessert."

It is an art and a science to be a good server. Believe me, they earn every penny of the tips. Can you imagine working a six- to eight-hours shift taking care of five to six tables at the same time - taking their orders, serving their foods, bringing whatever extra needs they want; then bringing their checks and giving back proper change? It is like playing four or five instruments at the same time, and all in different keys. Just try that some time.

Everyone has their own preferences on what great service is. But, as long as you walk away happy and contented, then your server has done their job. So, until the day comes when the servers are paid equally with the rest of the workers, and that no tipping is required, please have a heart for our dear server friends in the industry. We work very hard so you can have a smile on your face when you leave the restaurant. So, do the same for us, tip accordingly.

In search of happiness

W ell, we have finally settled down somewhat after moving up here a year ago. It is most amazing that my wife and I are happier now than we ever have been. Yes, we miss our friends in Milwaukee, and we miss all the restaurants with different concepts that we could frequently visit. Now, living in a smaller home, we are much happier than we ever have been. How can that be?

So, I started my journey in searching for happiness. And, surprisingly, none involves being rich, powerful or famous. And that hits me totally off guard, as growing up, I was molded to think that I have to work hard in order to make lots of money, have a career that can make me successful with a respectable status in the community and to live in a big mansion with a fancy car parked in the garage, just because. Just because of what? Till this day, I still don't know.

So, I started looking up various definitions of happiness, and this is what I found:

Happiness
- The quality of state of being happy
- Good fortune, pleasure, contentment, joy
- Exhilaration, bliss, contentedness, delight, enjoyment, satisfaction
- Pleasant and contented mental state
- Peace of mind
- Comes from warmheartedness
- Satisfaction with oneself
- By helping others
- More inner strength
- Fulfillment of one's purpose
- Sense of love
- Eliminate all ill feelings
- Being selfless
- Being positive
- Trusted friendships
- Families
- Companions

And, amazingly, fame and fortune were not even slightly mentioned. How strange indeed. Then I remembered an email a good friend sent me a while back. It was about a rich father who sent his son to live with a poor family for a while just to learn what it is like being poor. Upon his return, when the wealthy father asked how the trip was, this was his reply:

"We have one dog, and they have four. We have a pool that reaches to the middle of our lawn, and they have a creek that has no end. We have imported lanterns in our yard and they have stars at night. Our patio reaches to the front yard and they have the whole horizon. We have a small piece of land to live on, and they have fields that go beyond our sight. We have servants who serve us, but they serve others. We buy our food, but they grow theirs. We have walls around our property to protect us. They have friends to protect them." And then the boy added, "Thanks Dad, for showing me just how poor we are."

It is all based on one's perspective. Our happiness should be based on what we have and enjoying it, rather than worrying about what we do not have and what we have to do to achieve it.

And here is another story, from Arthur Ashe, the legendary Wimbledon player who was dying of AIDS, which he got from infected blood he received during heart surgery in 1983. He received letters from his fans, one of which conveyed, "Why did God have to select you for such a bad disease?"

Arthur Ashe replied, "The world over - 50 million children start playing tennis, 5 million learn to play tennis, 500,000 learn professional tennis, 50,000 come to the circuit, 5,000 reach the Grand Slam, 50 reach Wimbledon, four reach the semifinals, two reach the finals. And when I was holding the winning cup in my hand, I never asked God, 'Why me?' So now that I'm in pain, how can I ask God, 'Why me?'"

And I will end this week's column with the final words from Steve Jobs, the creator of Apple Computer, who passed away not too long ago.

LIFE

Steve Jobs' last words, or what he might have said

These words have been shown to not really be from Mr. Jobs as he was dying, but whoever wrote them, they are food for thought:

"As the CEO of a Fortune 500 company, I used to rebuke the business sector, invincible in the eyes of others. My life, of course, is a model of success. Now, in my hospital bed, I frequently think about my own life. I find that once I had a huge amount of pride in community fame and fortune but, in the face of impending death, all of this has become dull and meaningless.

"I repeatedly think about that late at night. What I want most now is something that my life's money and fame can never give me. What is it that has real value? In the dark, I look at those measuring machines, instruments with quiet green lights and buzzing sounds, and seem to feel death's warm breath move closer to me.

"Now, I understand that, as long as there is enough wealth in a man's life, the pursuit of other things, unrelated to wealth, should be the more important things, perhaps feeling, maybe it is art, maybe it is just a childhood dream. Endless pursuit of wealth will only make people greedy and boring.

"God made us, and gave us a rich sense of love in our hearts, rather than the sense of unreal wealth of money and fame. I won all the wealth I cannot take with me, and can take only memories of love and affection, which is the true wealth in life."

So, my dear friends, I have found my happiness. I hope you will find yours too.

Warm stories for cold evenings

A 4-year-old child's next-door neighbor was an elderly gentleman, who had lost his wife recently. The boy asked his mother if he could go visit his neighbor, who always brought him candies and fun toys. After spending a whole afternoon, he finally went home. Curious, his mother asked just what he did. He answered, "Nothing, Ma. I just helped him cry."

• • •

In Ms. Debbie Moon's class, the first-graders were sharing their family pictures. One little girl's picture stood out, as her skin and her family's were not the same. One boy blurted out, "So, are you adopted?"

Before she could answer, a little girl in the back raised her hand and said, "I know about adoption, I was adopted."

Now, more curious, Ms. Moon asked this little girl, "So, Marie, what does it mean to be adopted?"

"Well," Marie responded calmly, "My mommy told me that I grew in her heart instead of her tummy."

• • •

On my way home, I passed by a park where there was a Little League baseball game going on. I saw a little boy sitting excitedly on the bench. I couldn't help but find a place next to him and asked, "So, what's the score, son."

"14 to nothing," he exclaimed.

"14 to nothing. Who has 14?" Judging by his expression, I was anticipating that it was his team.

"They are 14, and we are nothing."

"What?" I asked myself, how could he be so excited about such a lopsided game? I couldn't help but asked him why he was so excited.

"Oh, I am next up to bat."

Talk about looking at life in a positive way. We have so much to learn from our children.

• • •

Little Jimmy Scott was so excited to participate at the school play. They had different auditions for different parts, but somehow little Jimmy was just not cut out for any theatrical part. Yet, one afternoon, he came home all excited. His mother, puzzled, asked what part he would be participating in. "The cheering and clapping part. I would be leading the audience," he exclaimed.

• • •

How about some turkey curry soup with sour cream topping for the cold evening? A good way to use up the leftover turkey from your Thanksgiving feast. This recipe serves four.

Turkey curry soup
- 8 oz. turkey, cubed
- 1 onion, diced
- 1 potato, diced
- 2 carrots, peeled and diced
- 1 can (8 oz.) coconut milk
- 1 can (8 oz.) evaporated milk
- 1 tsp chicken bouillon
- 1 tsp. garlic, minced
- 1 tbs. curry powder
- 4 tbs. sour cream

In a heated large pot, add 1 tbs. oil and minced garlic. Then add all vegetables and curry powder. Cook until potatoes and carrots are soft, then add coconut milk and evaporated milk. Then the cubed turkey, and bring it to a boil. You can add more milk to thin out the soup. Season to taste with chicken bouillon. Add a tablespoon of sour cream on top of each bowl and serve with steamed rice or buttered toast.

• • •

Remember the cartoon character Hagar the Horrible? He was teaching his son the art of shooting an arrow. After many tries, the arrows still missed the target by miles. Instead of getting frustrated and upset, he patted his son on the back and said, "It's great, son. All your arrows hit the ground."

Positive reinforcement 101.

•••
An eyewitness story:

A little boy, about 10 years old, was staring at a pair of warm shoes in the store window. An elderly lady, who was passing by, stopped and asked just what this shivering boy was doing, staring at the window. "Well, I was praying that God will give me a pair of shoes to warm my feet." Without saying a word, the lady took the boy inside, and asked the clerk to bring her some hot water. The clerk obliged immediately. The lady then helped the boy soak his feet in the warm water, and asked the clerk for some warm socks. After cleaning his feet and putting on some warm socks, they proceeded to get the boy the warmest boots. The boy was ecstatic and asked the elderly lady, "Excuse me, ma'am. Are you God's wife?"

LIFE

Cupping

We have terrible reception at our home. To use our cell phones to call others is like playing a game of chance, as the calls are often cut off in the middle of a conversation. And the landline is even worse. We have learned to go outside the house in order to get better reception. It is fine on a sunny day, but it is a different story when it is raining. Not to mention on a snowy day, which is coming soon.

In that sense, we seldom watch TV, as it takes a while to adjust the rabbit ears to point to the perfect direction before anything comes in. So, I caught the Olympic Games on the Internet and the newspapers instead. As always, the Americans have captured the most medals, and our athletes have shown pride and determination in their perfect performance. However, looking at the pictures of them receiving the medals on the podium, I couldn't help but noticing some big, round red marks on some of them. Especially Michael Phelps, the swimming beast, as he is lovingly addressed by his admirers. He was proudly showing his "cupping" marks to the world. So, what is this cupping about?

Then I read an article in the Chinese newspaper, proudly exclaiming that this ancient Chinese practice has now captured the attention of the whole world through the Olympic events, as athletes are proudly showing off their cup marks. So, just what in the world is cupping? Like acupuncture, the practice has been used by the Chinese for thousands of years. It seems far-fetched, how can one be cured by sticking a needle in your body in acupuncture? And now, this cupping?

Growing up in Hong Kong, I read a lot of Kung Fu novels and watched a lot of Kung Fu movies. They both featured something called "Dien Yeu," Touching Trigger Points, which was a powerful tool in offense and defense. There are thousands of trigger points in one's body, all connected to different blood vessels and lymph glands. And if those trigger points are attacked by force, the body will respond accordingly. And if the force is strong enough, it will stop the

165

blood flow immediately. And the person under attack would lose all mobility of his body. He would remain standing still, or just fall on the ground. Growing up, I was always mesmerized by the moves. To know "Dien Yeu," no bully would dare come close to me. Ha!

Acupuncture was introduced to the States in the '70s. Then slowly and surely, it was widely used by the NFL players. All claimed that the body pains caused by the hitting and punching were tremendously reduced after each treatment. In year 2002, there were over 5 million patients that had experienced the acupuncture treatment; and it has increased to 15 million these days. And now, most of the doctors are also using cupping with their acupuncture practice. So, how does acupuncture really work, sticking a fine needle into your body, how could that make you feel better?

I have a good friend in Milwaukee who is fascinated by the Chinese medicine. After college, he actually went to Texas to learn about the practice from a Chinese master. I have to give him a lot of credit, as he once showed me a chart of a human body, with thousands of dots and lines in different colors, connecting with each other. I have problems recognizing the names myself, but he fluently pronounced each one of them, in Chinese (though he doesn't read or write the language). "John, how did you do it?" I asked, totally amazed. "Well, you know that a lot of singers sing songs in different languages, without knowing the meaning of each word. Same here. Even though I don't know the meaning of each term, I know the sound of each word, and by connecting the different sounds, the whole picture is right in front of me." My right shoulder had been bothering me, from playing too much racquetball for years. After promising to buy him a couple of rounds of beer, he gave me a full demonstration.

First, he showed me what he learned from the master. There is this "chi," or air flow, in our body. Just like blood, it flows in our system. But somehow, when this chi is blocked by a clot of some sort, we will feel it by having body pain and spasm. And when a needle is placed in the trigger point, the clot is released, and the chi can flow freely again. And the pain is relieved. Totally amazing. And how would a non-

Chinese speaking American know all that? I am speechless, and a bit embarrassed.

The cupping is using the same principle, but with a different technique. It is rather simple. This holistic healing technology only requires some jars, either glass or plastic. The doctor would light a fire with cotton balls soaked in alcohol, and then place the fire inside the jar for about 30 seconds. Then he would place the jar upside down on the patient's back, moving it around for a bit. At times, three to four jars could be placed on different parts of the body. So, how does it really work? First, the doctor has to know just where those trigger points are located. When the cup is placed on the patient's body, it acts as a suction cup, drawing fresh blood and lymph into the area; increasing the blood flow and hence allowing the tissue to get more nutrients and oxygen. It reduces stiffness and muscle cramps. Also, it can remove scar tissue and help heal quicker. It relieves muscle aches and improves performance. Isn't that the dream and goal of each athlete?

Thanks to Michael Phelps promoting this wonderful treatment. Otherwise no one would ever know or believe that cupping is indeed a healing process, not just a trend, just like the introduction of acupuncture many years ago.

Chinese Pharmacies

Well, we have survived our first winter (I hope; after all, it is almost April). Before we moved to N.W. Wisconsin, our friends warned us about the miserable winters with blizzards which would bring 10 to 15 feet of snow. Thanks to El Nino, that never happened. And every day, we are counting our blessings:

• We are closer to our son's family in the Twin Cities. And we got to see our granddaughter much more often, watching her grow by the minute.

A collection of 1,000 medical herbs

• We have met many new friends – from the Book Club, our Church, and our neighbors (especially Irene and Robin across the lake). And from my writing classes, my barbershop (The Indianhead Chorus), and all my friends from the cooking classes....

• We got to watch the beautiful sunrise at the front porch and the sunset from our back porch every day, while listening to the rustling leaves, and hearing different birds serenading each other.

• I started to give cooking lessons and share my passion with others.

• We've discovered authentic Chinese restaurants and oriental stores in the Twin Cities (well, there are none on this side of the border).

We discovered this Dim Sum house in Bloomington which is quite authentic; and the discovery of different oriental grocery stores was an extra bonus. And, much to my surprise, one of the stores has a whole wall full of drawers from floor to ceiling, with a long glass counter in the front displaying colorful boxes of manufactured medicine. All of a sudden, the memories of my childhood in Hong Kong slowly resurfaced. What stood in front of me was an old fashioned pharmacy that I haven't seen for ages. And never in my wildest dreams would I expect to see one here.

I must have been 8 or 10 years old then. And in my old neighborhood, there was this herbal medicine store in the street corner. The first time I visited was when my mother sent me there to get some medicine for my brother who was not feeling well. When I entered the store, first thing I noticed was these drawers – they literally filled the whole back wall from top to bottom, and side to side. The drawers were the size of large shoe boxes, each labeled with an index card with Chinese writing. I recognized the words, but had no idea what they were. There was an elderly gentleman at the counter who asked me what I needed. So I repeated my mother's instructions: "My brother has a fever with an occasional cough. He doesn't have an appetite and doesn't sleep well at night." He paused and pondered for a minute, and then with separate bowls, he started opening the drawers, one at a time, and filled each one with the contents. A few times, he had to climb the ladder in order to get to the higher drawers. Then he gathered all the bowls; and from each bowl, he picked out the contents gently and weighed them carefully with his scale, which consisted of a long bamboo with markings, a dish hanging on at one end, and a movable weight at the other. Just by the way the scale was tilting, he knew he had the right amount of herb medicine (very scientific indeed). That went on with each ingredient. Then he gently put them all in a large piece of wax paper, and fold them neatly into a small package. Then he told me the cost, followed by the instructions. And just to be sure, he wrote them down on the package just in case. And lo and behold, my brother would feel better after a few days!

Herbal Medicine dates back 4,000 years in Chinese history. There was this fictional character Shen Nong who was supposed to have tasted many different herbs and plants and discovered which were beneficial or harmful to our bodies. Then, it was during the Ming Dynasty (1368 – 1644 A.D.) that a gentleman named Li Shizhen, who after spending 27 years of testing and collecting data, finally wrote a book on all the characters of the herbs, plants, flowers and roots that he researched. There were more than 1,800 of them. The most famous root drugs known in the U.S. are the Ginsengs, which are grown and harvested plentifully in Northern Wisconsin. Other medical plant such as Day Lilies, Chrysanthemums, Honeysuckle and Peonies, to name a few, are known more for their botanic beauty than their medical values.

My personal experience with Herbal Medicines was not the most pleasant, as most were bitter, pungent and hard to swallow. My mother had to bribe me with nuggets of candied fruit pieces before I would empty the bowl. But somehow, whatever I had and felt terrible, I felt better after a couple bowls of "Bitter Tea."

I admire those 'Herbal Pharmacists', who could memorize the characteristics of hundreds and thousands of these herbs, and also be able to cure one's illness by combining and mixing different herbs together. And while the Western doctors would use stethoscope to detect how one is breathing, or how one's heart is beating, the Eastern doctors could detect all that by putting his finger on your pulse. And in old days, when men and women were never to have physical contact, the doctors would attach a piece of string to the beating pulse, through a shaded curtain, and could diagnose whatever symptoms the patient behind the curtain had.

While we take different kinds of Vitamins to keep us healthy here in the Western world, the Chinese drink herbal teas which are supposed to clean your system. May be it is time for me to have a bowl of "Bitter Tea" now?

Itsy Bitsy Spider

Living in a log house in the North Woods, it is inevitable that we'll be sharing our home with many other animals and insects. After all, it has been their home for many, many years before we arrived. We were members of the Milwaukee County Zoo when we lived in Milwaukee. My wife loves animals, and we would spend hours watching different species roaming around in their 'natural' confinements. These days, we can watch them roaming around in their real natural environment around us; and best yet, no admission is required. What a concept!

I have to admit that most animals are very cute – the beavers building their dams; the turkeys marching through our back yard single file; geese flying in formation; and herds of deer roaming around the country roads (and yes, those pesky squirrels and the bears). These days, when we see an eagle circling above, it is not a spectacle anymore. Why get excited, when they are all over. But it is a sight to see when they glide around for a while, then all of a sudden dive into the water, and fly off with a fish still flipping & flapping. Now, that's entertainment! My wife has been around Robin (the Bird Man) for a while, and she can start naming different species and mimic the sound that they make. It is kind of fun to learn their names, their characters, their habits, and to recognize their tunes. Never realized that there are so many of them around.

My favorite time of the day is to sit on my back porch when the sun just rises; looking at the reflection of the lake; listening to the sound of the wind; and the different melodies from birds all around. I can identify some of the tweets and chirps from certain birds, while all gratifying and melodious, they are all varied. Sound of the wind, you might ask; is it possible?

Yes, definitely. When the wind passes by, it brushes the tall muscular trees with weaving leafy branches. The rustling sound is simply mesmerizing. Add the croaking calls from the shore- line frogs, with the occasional tee-hee-hee from the squirrels, it is nature symphony at its best. It is then that I would notice the newly weaved cob webs laced with morning dew, glistening in the morning sun. Didn't I just clean them all off yesterday?

Growing up in Hong Kong, we were warned to keep our house clean to avoid pests such as rats, cockroaches and spiders; as they carry disease that can make one sick. We learn to keep our homes clean by keeping trash and debris in proper containers that are sealed tight. The corners on the ceiling should be brushed with a broom often so no spiders could harbor there. Now these spiders are all over, what to do? When we first moved in, there were tiny cocoons all around the house. Later I found out that's where the eggs lived till they hatched. Needless to say, they were the first to go. Then there were cob webs along every corner. Took a while, but with a long broom, most were taken care of. The spiders went to hiding for a while, now every morning, they make their presence known again. Though it is most picture perfect – the sun beaming on the morning dew that cling gingerly on the web; it is truly a Kodak moment. Yet I've to do it, over and over again, morning after morning, to make them disappear.

My granddaughter loves to sing, yet 'Itsy Bitsy Spider' is not one of her favorites. As a matter of fact, she is totally scared of spiders. Wonder why?

"Itsy Bitsy Spider climbed up the water spout.
 Down came the rain and washed the spider out.
 Out came the sun and dried up all the rain.
 And the Itsy Bitsy Spider climbed up the spout again."

It is a harmless song indeed. Yet the lyrics remind me of our spiders – do what you want, but I'll be back again. There are a few favorite spots that the spiders would weave their webs, and every morning, I would brush the webs off. Yet, new webs would appear the next morning. How do they do it, and why, after all, knowing that it would be destroyed? Spiders are not dumb, as a matter of fact, they are one of the smartest hunters in the world. They have survived millions and millions of years before mankind came along, and have perfected all survival skills. Those spiders can fly, dive, swim, weave and dig. The only spiders that startled me is one tarantula in James Bond movie. Was it 'Dr. No'? The critter was climbing up my hero's arms before he brushed it off and smashed it to smithereens. The other one is the one from 'Lord of the Rings'. Mr. Frodo was stung by this monster tarantula, being wrapped up in a cocoon, just to be consumed later. Thank goodness 'Spider Man' came along. There's hope for mankind, after all.

Knowing how much work and how long it takes to weave a web, I've nothing but admiration about these 'Itsy Bitsy Spiders'. Wish I've the endurance to do what they do. If I have known that after spending tons of energy and lots of time to start a project, and at the same time knowing that there is a chance that someone would tear it apart completely, would I have the courage and patience to keep doing it? I am known to have no patience (hence, a lousy doctor, get it?) whatsoever. I know I won't be able to do it. However, after watching these "Itsy Bitsy Spiders', my thoughts have changed. Life is not about having the prettiest web, as it won't last forever. Life is about having faith, hope and belief in your dreams. That's what will keep us going. Ahh, so much to learn from these 'Itsy Bitsy Spiders'.

More on Itsy Bitsy Spider

I've written an article on Itsy Bitsy Spider earlier. It was a fun article, yet, there is more behind it that I want to share with you all. As much as they are a pest, yet spiders are really an admirable creature. What more, they've been living on earth before the dinosaurs roamed; long before we Homo Sapiens existed.

Yet, they just quietly do their own thing, never bother anyone, or even tried to offend anyone. Living in a log home, I've to be careful about their existence. As much as it is their habitat of building their webs in each corner of our home. Yet, I don't want to be at an 'Adam's Family' stage setting, living in an environment where cobwebs are everywhere, with a chaotic hand coming out of a deck box to play a tune or two to serenade me before I go to bed. Heavens, I've problems falling asleep the way it is. Worries? Not really, I am living in the North Woods, am I not?

My ritual every morning is to grab my teapot (with my favorite Jasmine Tea) and to sit at the deck to watch the sunrise. I would watch the sun slowly rising, and the dew drops glistening from my favorite flowers and plants. And that's when I notice the cobwebs at the corners. Didn't I just get rid of them the day before? What is it that they appear again, in the same pattern, with dew that glisten in the morning sun. I can't help but wonder, what's with these spiders? Why they keep doing the same thing over and over day after day, knowing that what they're doing will be destroyed again and again by a wild city boy?

Then it came to me about the human spiders. Yes, our heroes and celebrities who live among us with the spirits of the spiders. They kept pursuing the dreams, though over and over again, someone would come along and swept their beautiful webs away. I came across an article a while back, how a bunch of "successful" celebrities have gone through years of getting their web of dreams destroyed or turned away.

Yet, their spider spirits won't let it end. So what, I'll build another web, and it will be bigger and stronger. Just watch me. Oh, how I admire that little Itsy Bitsy Spider. I wish I have that courage and the endurance. What is failure? It is just a path to become a success, a stepping stone. Yet, how many of us would turn our backs on one tiny failure and feel sorry for ourselves, saying that we're just not good enough. So throw in the towels, give it up and move on to do other things that are better and meant to be. Dreams, goals, what are they? It won't work, and it never will, as that's what other people say, and that's what they think. No, not the spider, you can destroy my web, yet I'll be back next morning with a larger and better designed web. It might take me a long while, yet I'll be back, and I'll show you.

Every time I drive by a KFC store, looking at the portrait of an elderly colonel's smiling face; how I admire what he had done. A human spider he is indeed. Believing his recipes of 11 secret herbs and spices of doing his fried chicken, he carried his fryer and went around the country to search for an investor who would back up his growing plans. Do you know how many doors he knocked on, and each one turned him away, thinking that he was a crazy old fool? Ten, Twenty? No!? A hundred, five hundreds? Not even close. 1,009 times he knocked on investors' doors and each one turned him away. Yet the last one believed in him, and the rest is history. Talk about a human spider!

How about Walt Disney? His peers and superiors thought he lacked imaginations and had no good ideas. What? To make cartoons out of a mouse? Everyone sneered at his ideas and made fun of him. His webs were blown down and torn away for years and years. Even Disneyland was labeled to be a failure the day it was opened. He stuck to his dreams and just kept moving forward, weaving more webs and more webs. Now there are Disneyland in all parts of the world; and there isn't many kids who hasn't heard of Mickey Mouse.

Another human spider indeed.

How about Rocky, our boxing hero?

The creator Sylvestor Stallone had taken the script to different investors to get funding for producing the movie. No one believed in the story line. What? An unheard of boxing punk from Brooklyn challenging a boxing champ?

That was the craziest idea indeed. Yet, after 1,500 times of being turned down, he finally found a producer who believed in him and his story. Another human spider story? It is about the spirit of our spider friend.

Yes, you can destroy the web, but not the dream and the desire. How about Harry Potter, the wizard kid? The author and creator J.K. Rowlings had gone around to different publishers to sponsor her books. After the door was slammed shut twelve times, she finally had met someone who believed in her dreams. Another spider woman?

There are so many spiders living among us. Folks who believe in themselves and kept focusing on what they wanted to do than got discouraged when someone who kept knocking the webs down day after day.

Charlie Chaplain the tramp. Oh, how I love singing his song "Smile". It is another of my favorite besides "You'll Never Walk Alone."

Michael Jordan the basketball great, whose talent was ignored during his high school years.

How about Thomas Edison, who had tried 10,000 times before one invention worked.

And last of all, man I admire and respect, Abraham Lincoln.

His business failed; and he was demoted in the army; lost the presidential elections several times. Yet, with the spider spirits, he endured.

There is a little spider spirits in all of us.

We just have to dig it out ourselves. Keep spinning.

CHAPTER EIGHT: JOKES

Did you know?

Just when I thought I know everything, a good friend send me an email titled "Did you know?"
Well, he is retired, and his fun time is finding interesting articles on the Internet and sending them to his friends and family, whether they like it or not. Lucky me. Yet, some of the stuff he sends is quite interesting, so I want to share it with you, hoping that you enjoy it as much as I do.

• In the 1400s, a law was set forth in England that a man was allowed to beat his wife with a stick no thicker than his thumb. Hence we have the "rule of thumb."

• Many years ago in Scotland, a new game was invented. It was ruled "Gentleman Only ... Ladies Forbidden." And thus, the word GOLF entered into the English language.

• The first couple to be shown in bed together on prime-time TV were Fred and Wilma Flintstone.

• Coca-Cola was originally green.

• It is impossible to lick your own elbow.

• The cost of raising a medium-size dog to the age of 11 is $12,974 (or 10,120 British pounds).

• The first novel ever written on a typewriter was "Tom Sawyer."

• Each king in a deck of playing cards represent a great king from history:
Spades – King David, Hearts – Charlemagne, Clubs – Alexander the Great, Diamonds – Julius Caesar.

• $111,111,111 \times 111,111,111 = 12,345,678,987,654,321$.

• If a statue in the park of a person on a horse has both front legs in the air, the person died in battle. If the horse has one front leg in the air, the person died because of wounds received in battle. If the horse has all four legs on the ground, the person died of natural causes.

• Q: If you were to spell out numbers, how far would you have to go until you would find the letter A? A: One thousand.

• Q: What do bulletproof vests, fire escapes, windshield

wipers and laser printers have in common? A: All were invented by women.

• Q: What is the only food that doesn't spoil? A: Honey.

• In Shakespeare's time, mattresses were secured on bed frames by ropes. When you pulled on the ropes, the mattress tightened, making the bed firmer to sleep on. Hence the phrase … "Good night, sleep tight."

• It was the accepted practice in Babylon 4,000 years ago that for a month after the wedding, the bride's father would supply his son-in-law with all the mead he could drink. Mead is honey beer and because their calendar was lunar-based, this period was called the honey month, which we know today as the honeymoon.

• In English pubs, ale is ordered by pints and quarts. In old England, when customers got unruly, the bartender would yell at them, "Mind your pints and quarts and settle down." It is how we get the phrase: "Mind your P's and Q's."

• Many years ago in England, pubs frequently had a whistle baked into the rim, or handle, of their ceramic cups. When they needed a refill, they used the whistle to get some service. "Wet your whistle" is the phrase inspired by this practice.

• Can you lick your elbow??

More fun stuff
You know you are living in 2017 when:

1. You accidentally enter your PIN on the microwave.

2. You haven't played Solitaire with real cards in years.

3. You have a list of 15 phone numbers to reach your family of three.

4. You email the person who works at the desk next to you.

5. Your reason for staying in touch with friends and family is that they don't have e-mail addresses.

6. You pull up in your own driveway and use your mobile phone to see if anyone is home to help you carry in the groceries.

7. Every commercial on TV has a website at the bottom of the screen.

8. Leaving the house without your mobile phone, which you didn't even have before (assuming you are in your 50s or 60s), is now a cause for panic. You actually will turn around

to get it.

10. You get up in the morning and go online, before getting your coffee.

11. You start tilting your head sideways to smile :)

12. You are actually nodding and agreeing, and laughing, right now.

13. You did not notice that there is no No. 9 on this list.

Ha ha ha, laugh yourself silly. Life is too short. Have a little fun and enjoy the journey.

Talk about having a little fun, here are a few jokes that I would like to share with y'all": enjoy!!

• • •

A man and a woman were sharing a first-class cabin on a long journey. While the lady was enjoying reading her book, the guy was talking to his wife on the phone the minute the train left the depot. He was telling his wife what he had for breakfast, the details of his business meetings, and the accommodations of the different hotels that he stayed in. It went on for hours, and the guy was talking freely and loudly, having a grand time. Finally, the lady had enough. She went over to the guy, grabbed his phone, and said, "Honey, can you come back to bed?" and then went back to her seat.

It was silence all the way to their destination.

• • •

An elderly gentleman visited the jewelry store with his young love interest. She was looking at rings and necklaces. Finally she found a bracelet that she liked, and the price tag was $35,000!

Without blinking an eye, the elderly gentleman approached the owner and said, "Sir, I do not carry that much cash on me. But I'll give you a check for $35,000, which you can cash on Monday, after I transfer my funds. I'll come and pick up the bracelet when the account is clear." Deal was done, and everyone was happy. Come Monday, the owner was furious, finding out that the account didn't have enough money to cover the purchase. He called the elderly gentleman, and he calmly replied, "Yes, I know that I don't have enough money in the account. But let me tell you what a wonderful weekend I had."

Hope you are laughing. And how does that elbow of yours taste?

Jokes

The owner of a gold mine in California had to go on a business trip. Before he left, he called three of his trustworthy employees together, "Gentlemen, I will be gone for a few weeks and I would like you to keep business as usual. Hans, you are very organized, please make sure all the payroll is done and keep the books in order."

"Jawohl," replied Hans, "No problem."

He then turned to Pierre, who was an excellent chef, "Pierre, can you make sure that all the employees are fed everyday with your great food?"

"Oui, monsieur, will do," said Pierre.

Finally, he looked at Wong Fu and said, "Now, can you take care of all the supplies?"

"Oh, I like supplies, no problem," replied Wong Fu.

The owner was gone for a few weeks, and upon his return, he found that Hans did a good job taking care of payroll and the books, and Pierre had indeed cooked great meals for all employees. He was pleased. However, they couldn't locate Wong Fu. So, they went looking for him. And while passing a dark tunnel, out jumped Wong Fu from the corner, he waved his arms and shouted excitedly, "Supplies!"

• • •

A bunch of tourists visited Chinatown in New York City for the first time. They were impressed to see live fish sold in the fish market and roasted ducks hanging by their necks at the barbecue deli. Then at the corner of Main Street, they saw the sign "Abramov Laundromat." Curious, they went inside just to find that, besides doing laundry, the owner sold coffee cups, T-shirts and baseball caps with the logo Abramov Laundromat, NYC on them. Apparently, he was doing quite well. They asked for the owner, wanting to know more about his success. A Chinese gentleman showed up, and said he was the owner. Now, more confused, the tourists wanted to know how a Chinese guy ended up with a name Abramov.

180

"Ah, I came to America on boat many years ago. Many, many people on boat and long, long line at immigration office. Officers very, very tired. When gentleman before me checked in, they asked,

"Wot your name?" "Abramov," he replied. "Good, next." Then he asked me, "Wot your name?" I said, "Sam Ting."

• • •

I had a colonoscopy checkup more than 10 years ago. I know that even though it is a drag, I need to do it again. So, I got myself an appointment. While in the doctor's office, I noticed something different. On his prep station there was a tube of KY jelly, some plastic surgery gloves and a bottle of beer. Being curious, when the doctor entered the room, I told him that I recognized the tube of jelly and the gloves, but what's with the beer? He stormed out the office and slammed the door. I could hear his voice in the other room, "Marie, I thought I told you that I would need a butt light."

• • •

Overhearing a wife's praying at night:
"Lord, please give me the wisdom so I can understand my husband, to understand his swinging moods, and his constant needs and wants. Give me the patience, so I know how to handle and put up with his erratic behaviors. And Lord, please don't give me strength, for I will strangle him."

• • •

A preacher wanted to show his congregation the evil of smoking and drinking. So he conducted an experiment. He put together three jars – one filled with alcohol, one filled with tobacco and the other one with good old dirt from the garden. Then he put a worm in each jar. On Sunday, he brought them to the church and in front of his congregation, he opened the jar filled with alcohol, just to find that the worm was dead. Then he opened the jar filled with tobacco, lo and behold, it was dead, too. He then proceeded to open the one that was filled with dirt and the worm was wiggling, filled with life.

He smiled, and addressed the congregation, "So, you see here, right in front of you, the evil of smoking tobacco and drinking alcohol. What do you think of that"?

In the back came a small voice from an elder lady, "I got it, if you keep drinking alcohol and smoke tobacco, you will never get worms."

• • •

As a professor was teaching a nutrition class, he was expressing his thoughts on how unhealthy our foods have become. "Meat has been injected with hormones and are being fed chemicals. Our beverages are made with artificial sweeteners. Fruits and vegetables are sprayed with pesticides and artificial fertilizers. And how about Chinese foods?

They are loaded with MSG that can give you headaches and heartburns." He paused, looked around, and said, "Now, who can tell me what other foods can cause constant headaches and heartburn?"

An elderly gentleman in the front raised his hand and softly said, "Wedding cake."

• • •

There was an essay contest and the winner could win $10,000. The topic was, What is the difference between complete and finished?

One gentleman turned in his definition in less than fifteen minutes. All the judges voted that he was indeed the winner with the best explanations. Here is what he wrote:

"When you marry a perfect woman, your life is complete. However, when you are caught cheating by this perfect woman, you are finished."

• • •

A case of beer holds 24 cans ... And there are 24 hours in a day.

I love reading jokes, it's fun that we are able to laugh at silly stuff in life and, more importantly, to be able to laugh at ourselves. After all, laughter is the best medicine, right? My wife and I had been going around nursing homes when we were living in Milwaukee, serenading the seniors. Many of them were in wheelchairs and didn't have much mobility. Yet, I could still see them tapping their toes or moving their fingers while we sang. I loved to tell them jokes, I knew they enjoyed them by the hint of their smile and the nod of their heads (for my approval, at least, while my wife would just roll her eyes). Life is too short and if telling jokes can make someone happy, I'll keep telling.

So, here they are:

• • •

A guy went to a bar and order three shots of whiskey. The bartender was baffled, and said, "Sir, why three separate shots? I can put them all in one glass for you."

The guy said, "No, you don't understand. When I drink, I want to share the toast with my two brothers. You see, I live in Wisconsin, but I have a brother who lives in New York, and another in California. So, each time when I drink, I am sharing that with them too." The bartender gladly obliged. Each time he showed up, there would be three shots waiting for him.

And it went on for months. Then, one day, the guy came in and told the bartender to just pour two shots instead of three. Puzzled, the bartender asked, "Hey, why two shots instead of three, as usual?"

The guy replied, "Ahh, I quit drinking."

• • •

A wife is looking at the mirror one morning, and then complained to her husband, "Honey, look, everything is falling apart. I got wrinkles in my eyes. And look at these muscles, they are getting flabby and saggy. Everything is going south."

Without blinking an eye, the husband said, "Oh, babe, your eyesight is as good as ever."

And he is still in the hospital.

• • •

An avid golfer is curious about life in heaven after death, so he went to a fortune teller to find out if there is golfing in heaven. The fortune teller looked at the crystal ball and then said, "Yes, there are plenty of golf courses in heaven.

All beautifully trimmed and maintained. You can be golfing eternally. But I see just one minor handicap."

"What is it?" The golfer inquired.

"Well," the fortune teller said, "Your tee time is at 8:30 a.m. tomorrow."

JOKES

•••

This guy lived in a high-rise apartment in Manhattan. One morning, to test out how the weather was going to be for the day, he reached his hand outside the window and waited. Then, lo and behold, there was a "splat" in his palm. He was surprised to find that it was a glass eye. Not knowing where it came from, he stuck his head out the window, and saw a beautiful lady two floors up waving at him, signaling him to bring the eye back to her.

He went up to her place and she invited him to stay for some cocktails. They chatted and had a good time. As time flew, he was getting hungry and she said, "Why don't you stay for dinner. I have something warming up in the oven already."

He stayed, and they had dinner and some wine. It was a delightful evening indeed. Then, as he was leaving to go back to his own place, she invited him to spend the evening with her. A little taken back, he said, "Excuse me, but do you do that with everyone?"

And she said, "No, only with the ones that catch my eye."

•••

God created Adam, and he was quite happy in paradise. But, somehow, he got lonely, and went to God and complained that he wanted some company. God was very accommodative, He said, "Adam, I can make you this perfect woman. She will be kind, gentle and obedient, never to question you, and she will do whatever you want and whatever pleases you to keep you happy."

Adam was elated. "God, thank you, thank you. What do I have to do?"

And God said, "It will cost you an arm and a leg."

"An arm and a leg? That's way too much. So what if I just give a rib?"

And that's how Adam got Eve for a rib.

•••

Pastor John died and went to heaven. St. Peter met him at the Pearly Gates and welcomed him. "Brother John, welcome. Let me show you to your eternal resting place." So, he was shown a nice apartment with lots of sunlight and room, it was a good resting place indeed. As they were walking out, he saw this big beautiful mansion, with manicured garden, swimming pool, and tennis court. He was flabbergasted, and asked St. Peter, "Wow, this is some place to live. Who lives there, God himself"?

And St. Peter said, "No, this is the place for Tony, a taxi driver at New York City."

Pastor John was dumbfounded, and said, "Wait, I preached at our church all my life, Sunday after Sunday. And all I got is to live in this tiny apartment? And this taxi driver Tony from New York City got to live in this beautiful, wonderful mansion? What gives?"

St. Peter calmly explained. "Brother John, here in heaven, we measure everything by results, and not just efforts. Yes, you work very hard, preaching every Sunday for many, many years. You have indeed devoted your life to the mission of God. But yet, when you preach, everybody falls asleep.

But now, when Tony drives his taxi around New York City, everybody prays."

A message indeed of efforts and results.

• • •

A guy went to the local diner, and told the waitress that he wanted a "quickie." Embarrassed, she slapped him in the face and stormed away. The guy was shocked and didn't know what to say or do. Then an elderly gentleman who sat behind his booth turned around and said, "Mister, I think you meant to say 'quiche.'"

• • •

A dad went to the toy store to buy a Barbie doll for his daughter's birthday. And holy smoke, there were all kinds of Barbie dolls - skier Barbie, surfing Barbie, singer Barbie, ... and the prices ranged from $15 to $25. Then he came across a divorced Barbie, and the price tag was $150. Amazed, he asked the owner why such a big price difference. Then the owner explained, "Well, a divorced Barbie comes with Ken's sports car, a regular house, plus a beach home."

• • •

On the way to the airport, the passenger forgot something, so he gently tapped the taxi driver on the shoulder in order to ask him. The driver let out a loud scream, and swerved along the road, barely missing the oncoming traffic, and finally stopped at the sidewalk. The passenger apologized to the driver, that he startled him. "No, it is my fault," the driver exclaimed. "I just started driving this taxi not too long ago. I was a hearse driver. And for 35 years, no one had ever tapped on my shoulder before."

• • •

A blind gentleman just received a Seeing Eye dog to guide him around. He was told that the dog was well-behaved and well-trained. So, the gentleman took him for a walk around the neighborhood for a test. As soon as the dog saw a stray cat on the sidewalk, he went berserk and went after the cat, dragging the blind gentleman behind. They knocked over a newsstand and a hot-dog vendor before they finally came to a stop. The poor guy was barely catching his breath, while he reached into his pocket and pulled out a dog treat for the dog. A pedestrian who witnessed the whole incident was baffled, and asked the blind gentleman, "Excuse me, sir, I saw the whole thing. This dog almost got you killed, and you're giving him a treat?" "No, this is not really a treat. I just want to find out where his mouth is, so I can kick his other end."

• • •

A husband got into a bad accident, and his face got badly burnt. The doctor said that he could perform surgery to save his disfigured face, but he would need a skin graft from a compatible donor. As in a miracle, the tests showed that the skin from his wife's buttock was a perfect match. The wife, who wanted to save her husband, gladly obliged. The operation was a huge success. Not only did the husband look much younger, but he also became more handsome than before. The husband was most grateful, and asked the wife what he could do for her in return. The wife calmly exclaimed,

"No honey, I love you, and there's no need for being thankful. Anytime I see your mother kissing your face, that's my reward."

Points to ponder:

How come they put artificial lemon flavors in our drinks, but put real lemons in the dish detergent?

How come the drugstores make a sick person walk all the way to the back counter to get their prescriptions, yet cigarettes are sold at the front counter?

How come mosquito bites are driving me crazy, but as soon as I pick up the lotion that stops the itches, all itching stops.

Military jokes:

Two privates wanted weekend passes. The sergeant asked the first private, "Why would you need a weekend pass?" "To help my pregnant wife, Sir." "And how about you?" he asked the second private. "To help my wife get pregnant, Sir." They both got their passes.

• • •

A young man was overheard telling his buddies, "I am so tired of everyone telling me what to do all the time. As soon as I graduate, I am out of here and will join the Marines."

• • •

The sergeant was really impressed with this new recruit who followed orders and excelled in all his assignments. "Son," he asked the young man, "Do you have any previous experience in the service?" "No, Sir," said the soldier, "I grew up with three older sisters."

• • •

A captain took his wife out for a fun evening in his uniform.

And when they entered the theater, the crowd cheered and gave them a standing ovation. Pleased, he smiled and waved back. After the show was over, an audience member approached them and thanked them. Being humble, he said that it wasn't necessary for such a kind gesture. "No, that was wonderful of you and your wife to show up. We only had 13 people here, and the owner of the theater said that there would be no show till we have 15 paying customers. And then you two showed up."

• • •

The young daughter of a Navy SEAL was showing her class what her daddy does. After the show and tell, a sweet young girl approached the proud dad and asked, "Sir, can you balance a ball on your nose?"

• • •

Talking about getting lost in translation, here is one from English to Russian and back:

"The spirit is willing, but the flesh is weak." – English
"Vodka horosho, no mayaca slabie." – Russian
"The alcohol is good, but the meat is terrible." – translation from Russian to English

• • •

A retired colonel wanted to keep busy after his retirement, so he decided to get a civilian job. However, he had problems about being on time every morning. The manager liked his work, but had to talk to him about his punctuality. "Mr. Johnson, at your previous job, what did people say to you when you walked in late?" "Oh, the usual," the retired colonel replied, "would you like some coffee now, Sir?"

• • •

In a Spanish class, the professor was explaining to the class that, in Spanish, all nouns are designated as either male or female. House, for instance, is feminine, "la casa," same with door, which is also feminine, "la puerta." However, train is considered masculine, "el tren," so is pencil, "el lapiz." A student in the back row asked, "El professor, so what is the gender of a computer? Should it be 'el computadore,' or 'la computadora?'"

Instead of giving the answer, the professor divided the class into two groups, male and female, and asked them to decide for themselves what gender the computer should be, masculine or feminine. And each group was asked to give four reasons for its recommendation.

The male group decided that the computer should definitely be of the feminine gender because:

• No one but their creator understands their internal logic.

• The native language that is used to communicate with other computers is incomprehensible to everyone else.

• Even the smallest mistakes are stored in long-term memory for possible later retrieval.

• As soon as you make a commitment to one, you find yourself spending half your paycheck on accessories for it.

The female group somehow concluded that the computers should definitely be masculine because:

• In order to do anything with them, you have to first turn them on.

• They have a lot of data but still can't think for themselves.

• They are supposed to help you solve problems, but half of the time they are the problem.

• As soon as you commit to one, you realize that if you had waited a little longer, you could have gotten a better model.

Guess which side won?

• • •

A lady brought her sick pet parakeet to the vet for a checkup. The vet took a look and shook his head. He told the lady that the pet was at its final days. The lady insisted on a second opinion. So the vet called in his Labrador. He smelled and sniffed the bird, shook his head and left. However, the lady insisted on having another opinion. So the vet called in his cat. He, too, smelled and sniffed the bird, shook his head and left. Devastated, the lady asked for the bill. The vet presented a bill of $1,050. The lady was in awe, "$1,050, that's ridiculous. Why so expensive?"

"Well, my bill was just $50. But, with the Lab test and the cat scan, that's how much it cost."

• • •

An elderly gentleman went for his regular checkup and told the doctor that God has been good to him. Every evening when he went to the bathroom, the light would go on when he opened the door. And, poof, it would go off by itself when he was done. Totally amazed, the doctor asked his wife, who accompanied him, if that was the case. "No, that old fool," the wife exclaimed, "he has been peeing in the refrigerator."

• • •

I heard that somewhere:

"When I feel a pain in my knee, I know that the rain is coming; when I feel a pain in my neck, I know a relative is coming"

"Getting old is like visiting an all-you-can eat buffet; what's supposed to be hot is cold, what's supposed to be firm is limp and the buns are the biggest among everything."

"I love cooking with wine; sometimes I like to add some to the food."

• • •

A young, beautiful lady boarded a plane to New York City.

Even though her ticket was for economy class, she decided to take a seat in first class when she saw an opening. The stewardess tried to explain to her that she had to move back to her own ticketed seat. Apparently, being spoiled and getting her own way her whole life, she refused to budge. The stewardess had no choice but to ask the captain for help. The co-pilot overheard the conversation and said that he would handle it. He went straight to the beautiful lady and whispered something in her ear. She smiled, and immediately stood up and moved back to her original seat. Dumbfounded, the captain asked the co-pilot what he said to her. "Oh, nothing really. I just told her that first class does not fly to New York City."

• • •

In a "Who Wants To Be A Millionaire" show the contestant was asked this question: What bird does not build its own nest?

A. Robin, B. Sparrow, C. Cuckoo and D. Thrush.

The contestant was stuck. Not knowing what to do, she used the lifeline to call her best friend, Maggie. Without even pondering, Maggie said, "It is the cuckoo." Trusting her best friend's intuition, she gave the host the final answer, the cuckoo. Bells went off and lights were twirling, and she won a million dollars for the correct answer.

Later, she called Maggie just to find out how she knew the answer. This is what Maggie said: "It is easy, we all know that cuckoo lives in a clock."

Do not ever judge people by the color of their skin or the color of their hair.

CHAPTER NINE: BUSINESS

The six Ps of starting a business

A few weeks ago, I was invited to give a lecture to the business class in Spooner High School. The students are mostly juniors and seniors. They have to prepare a business plan in how to start a business. I gladly obliged, as being a business consultant, I have been giving advice to business owners in how to start and operate a business for many years. It is amazing that I found Spooner on the map. A man known to have no sense of directions, it took me a while to realize that Osceola is south of where we live, and Luck and Frederic are on the north end. Taylor Falls is on the west, and to reach Amery, I have to go east, and then go south on 46. And Spooner is way, way farther north, 45 minutes farther north of Turtle Lake. Living in Milwaukee all these years, I was used to traffic jams. And driving more than 15 minutes to reach my destination was considered "long distance." Now, I can drive 50 miles without seeing a living soul (cattle, yes). And an hour drive is considered fair game. Ah, so much to adjust to, but I'm loving it.

Anyway, talking to those young students brings back memories. They know just enough about supply and demand; but yet, they clearly understand why McDonald's is offering a $1 meal just to get you in the door, and then will sock you with a $2 soda or a $3 bag of fries, which cost them 15 to 20 cents. Smart kids indeed. Can't help but love them.

So, I wrote six P's on the board. And asked them what the P's stand for before they actually open a business. And lo and behold, they got them all. Now, I wish all the business owners I dealt with before would have talked to these kids before they opened their business. Yes, there is future for our next generation!

So, what are the six P's? They are Price, Place, People, Product, Promotion and Profit. They named them all, and needless to say, I was speechless. Wow! So let's talk about each P, and why it is so important.

Price: Golden rule – charge too much, no customer will buy. But don't charge enough, you work for free. It is a science to be competitive and stay in business at the same time. But as long as you're being honest and consistent, and serve a good product, folks are willing to pay the price.

Place: Like the old saying, "location, location, location." Is the business in an area that is visible to traffic, or it is hidden somewhere inside the mall? Is there ample parking? And how about the rent? How much products would you need to serve every day in order to pay rent? Most of the rents are 3 percent to 5 percent of the sales. The ideal location is away from the madding crowd with cheaper rent, but customers will find you because you have a unique product.

People: Who are your customers? In the past, I taught students about Demographics and psychographics of the guests. Demographics is something that you actually see, like their race. Are they black, white, green, yellow or red? Their age, how old are they? What other features that you can notice? Psychographics is a bit difficult to recognize – their religion, their profession, their status seeking ... Having a BBQ wood pit restaurant serving famous ribs and pork shoulder in a Jewish or Muslim neighborhood spells disaster. We have to spend some time studying our neighbors – who are they? Will they spend money on our products continuously? And then, who are your employees? How are you going to teach and train them so they can become a "mini you"?

Product: Again, what is our niche? Are we serving something that the customers will like? Or serving something that we hope they will like? And what makes our products so different that they will come back and try us over and over? How many pizzerias are there in your town? And why would you go back to the same one over and over again? Despite the price that they charge and their location? We have to think outside the box and serve something totally unique and different from the competitors. And that's not just foods we are talking about. How about watches, clothing, shoes, or whatever, what makes your product different?

Promotion: Do you remember how much it costs to

advertise at the Super Bowl for a 30-second spot? Millions! But big companies are willing to pay, because people watch. Whether they will buy or not is another story, but they watch, and they know the product exists! We can spend zillions of dollars advertising and promoting, but does it work? A good friend who is a banker once told me that to get a new customer to open a new account with their branch, it costs them between $500 to a $1,000 in advertising. Come to think of it, there are billboard ads which cost $1,000 to $2,000 a month pending on the locations. Newspaper and magazine ads are extremely costly. And TV, ha-ha, unless you're the auto companies who can spend $100,000 for a 30-second ad. So, what can you do to bring in more customers? I've taught many business owners that to get loyal, returned customers costs them nothing. Yet, they have to be "the host with the most."

Like most people, I pay my bill with my credit/debit card. What if when the server returned my card, they said, "Thank you, Mr. Kwong, come back and see us soon." (My name is on the card!) And if the owner calls me by my name when I was leaving, I would be his friend for life! So, spending thousands and got nothing? Or spending nothing and get thousands?

Profit: Why are we in business? To make a profit. To pay bills and to have a life. We need a P&L (profit and loss statement) to know where we stand so we can make continuous adjustments in order to survive. Why stay in business if we are not making money?

Anyway, hats off to my young Spooner friends. Our future depends on them.

Total customer satisfaction

Just when I was running out of ideas about writing the column, I asked my buddy Dave Muller for help. He is in my writers class and book club, a true friend indeed.

Many years ago, my wife and I were discussing who we should consider as true friend. Yes, we have many associates whom we either work with, or know from church or through other organizations. But who are your true friends? So, after many hours of pondering the thought, we came up with this definition – a true friend is someone you can call at 3 a.m. and ask them to pick you up at the airport just because. No explanations are needed. You're stranded and you need help.

And a true friend would get up, mumble a few bad words, then would get in the car to pick you up, no matter where you are, without asking why you ever got into the mess to start with. Am I correct with the definition?

Anyway, knowing that I'm in the food business, David's advice for my column is to write about good/poor service, food presentation, memorable employees, stories of training chefs, what makes a good restaurant, why so many restaurants fail, food and menus that surprise me, and how food unites us and makes events and holidays extraordinary. Holy smoke, all these will keep me busy for a few months.

So, let's talk about service first. What's considered good or poor service? Have you ever been to a restaurant where the dining tables are sticky? You rest your arm on the table and you have a problem lifting it afterward. Salt and pepper shakers are half filled and smeared with grease. And worse, the salt is mixed with black pepper. Looks like a bunch of dead ants in the salt shaker.

After you're seated, the host would show you a menu stained with dry ketchup and mutter, "Enjoy your meal."

Would you? Good service is not just about taking your orders and then serving your food when it's cooked. It is the whole dining experience. Based on my consulting experience, the whole perception starts from the parking lot.

Is the parking lot clean and swept, or still littered with beer bottles and trash from last night's party? Are the restaurant's lights on? How about the sign? Is it well-lit for all to see?

The front door, especially if it is a glass door, is it clean and shiny, with no smeared fingerprints? Are you greeted by an employee immediately? Or do you stand there watching the world go by?

When you're finally seated, does the server approach you right away and say something like, "Welcome, let me take care of a few things and I'll be right with you." Or rather, run circles around you and never even address your presence? It's happened to me many times. Knowing that the server was busy, yet, passing me by several times, but never saying "boo."

And then finally, upon approaching our table, the first thing that he/she said would be, "Are you ready to order now?" I know many of us have experienced that before. And is that the assumption of a total dining experience? Absolutely not. But, it happens in many restaurants these days, still. And I wonder how they keep on operating.

Yes, I agree, operating a fast-food joint and a regular restaurant are a little different, yet the bottom line should still be the same – total customer satisfaction. Many years ago, the National Restaurant Association did a survey on customer satisfaction – what are the expectations of the customers? A lot of little things, but they add up, including convenient location, good food/unique food, moderate/affordable price, warm service with a smile, clean bathrooms, clean environment including counter, tables and chairs, floors and kitchen, and a well-lit and clean parking lot.

We don't ask for much, do we? All basic operational stuff, besides the convenient location. But I'm surprised to find out that a lot of operations can't even keep up with that. I was at a burger fast-food place recently to catch a quick bite. The place was busy but not packed, yet it was chaotic. It was around lunchtime, and they had employees loaded in the front and back, 10 at least, five in the front and five in the back. There were two customers in front of me. "Good," I thought to myself, "I should be out of here in no time flat, just grab my food and go." At least that was my optimistic thinking.

Apparently the cashier was still in training or just came out of training. After each order he punched in, he had to pause and ask the manager, who was wearing a tie and a different color shirt, for approval. And then he hit the wrong payment key, and would have to start the order all over again.

Meanwhile, a customer who picked up his order claimed it wasn't what he ordered. Someone must have picked up the wrong food and the whole order had to be recooked again. So, to right the wrong, everything was put on hold till the messed-up order was cleared. After what felt like an eternity, I was still behind two customers waiting for my turn to order. And then, the worker in charge of the specialty coffee department blurted out loudly to the manager, "Can you tell Johnny to fill up the machine. I can't do anything when the machine is almost empty."

All the employees were busy doing something, but I was still behind two customers. The parking lot is clean, and so is the bathroom, at least the men's. But what would you think about my customer service experience? Needless to say, I left and went to get a brat sandwich in a nearby gas station instead.

So, what are your expectations on total customer satisfaction?

More on customer satisfaction

You have probably read about the latest on United Airlines, how a customer was dragged out of his seat and carried by force to leave the plane from the seat that he had booked and checked in accordingly. He refused because he wanted to be home. All the airline wanted to do was to get four seats for the employees who had to make connections to other cities.

The plane was overbooked, yet no one wanted to give up their seats, the airline even offered free tickets with food and hotel accommodations. Been there and done that. Did a lot of traveling in my younger days with my consulting business. When I was gone for three to four weeks at a time, I had to be back home on a certain date and at a certain time. Many times, I would go directly from the airport to attend my kids soccer or softball game, a birthday party, teachers' conference, or a singing recital or a play my kids were in. Missing any of those would mean instant death. A free hotel accommodation with dinner sounded good but the price that I would have to pay was not worth it. Just to think of what would happen if my daughter couldn't find me in the spectator stand when she was playing the state finals soccer game. Yes, her expression didn't show it but she could spot me miles away. To miss my son's recital would be another deadly sin. For some strange reasons, my kids could always spot me.

I don't know anything about the passenger that was dragged away, he had his reasons and I can relate to whatever his reasoning was – "I need to be home." Yet, from the airline's standpoint, it was that they had the right to remove any passengers they desired to accommodate their needs. So, where does customer service come in? In a sense, they want to boast about their customer service, achieving total customer satisfaction and gaining customer loyalty. "Fly the friendly skies," they say. Yet, before you hit the sky, you hit the floor first, being pulled out of the plane against your will, with blood streaming down your face, screaming for help. Just how friendly can one get?

After the incident, a lot of folks came out with these funny lines, which I want to share with you. It is funny in a sense, but how sad is it for the hospitality industry? Being in the hospitality industry all these years, total customer satisfaction is our utmost goal; do what you can to make the customer happy. But now, there are new mottos for United Airlines:

- We put the hospital in hospitality.
- Board as a doctor, leave as a patient.
- Our prices can't be beaten, but our passengers can.
- We have First Class, Business Class and No Class.
- Not enough seating, prepare for a beating.
- We treat you like we treat our luggage.
- We beat our customers, not our competition; or: If we can't beat our competition, we beat our customers.
- And you thought leg room was an issue.
- Where voluntary is mandatory.
- Fight or flight? We decide.
- Now offering one free carry off.
- Beating random customers since 2017.
- If our staff needs a seat, we'll drag you out by your feet.
- A bloody good airline.

Even United Airlines stated over and over that it is their policy and they reserve the right to do what it takes to keep the company operating effectively and efficiently. That kind of leaves me wondering – just what are your business guidelines? How can any business survive without any customers? Now with this incident, how can one retain any customer loyalty? Knowing that I might be dragged away if the circumstances arise again, do you think I will fly the friendly skies ever again? While apologizing profoundly about the incident, the president and CEO still hinted that those employees were doing the right thing. Just what has total customer satisfaction come to?

Living up here in the North Woods, we have our share of frustrations with customer service. For some services, there are no competitors so, their motto seems to be "put up or shut up." There is an Internet company that we use that we are not happy with at all:

- The dish that they installed fell off the roof, taking the ceiling attached.

- They always put us on hold forever when we tried to call.
- They have no record of the conversation of what they promised.
- The billing was wrong every month.

Yet, they kept sending me survey of what we think of their service. What to do?

Companies would spend hundreds and thousands of dollars to get new customers. According to to the Small Business Administration, their survey indicates that most companies would spend between $500 to $1,000 to gain a new customer. Yet, 68 percent or more customers leave because they feel that they are not being treated right. Customers are willing to pay more for excellent service, yet most companies are still pondering just what good service is. At the same time, they are so focused on bottom-line profit: Are we making money, how can we increase sales and cut back on expenses so we can make more money? All these questions are raised by presidents and CEOs who make a zillion dollars a year. They can't see the answers that are right in front of their eyes - total customer satisfaction is the key. Achieving that is simple and easy: customer service and customer satisfaction to gain customer loyalty.

It is so easy to achieve, yet why ignored by so many? I am a consumer and I just want to be happy after spending the money. If I have a complaint, listen to it and fix it. Hear about my concerns, my problems and show me that you CARE: Communicate, Acknowledge, Respect and Empathize. I am not asking for free this and that, I just want a fair and square deal. How United Airlines can quote the "Fly the friendly skies" again will take some time. How they are going to tie that with total customer satisfaction will take more time.

Hello? Is anyone listening?

Identity theft

A month ago, I got a letter from a credit adjuster company asking me to please call them to settle an account. Being curious, I called the number that they gave to find out what it was all about. The operator, being courteous, asked me to verify who I was; that I was the right person that they were talking with. So, I gave them my name and my address. It was when she asked me for my birth date and Social Security number that I got suspicious and hung up. Why would anyone want to know that personal information over the phone? It was a recurring nightmare that I thought had gone away.

When we were living in Milwaukee, I got this letter about settling a loan with a certain company, even with a case number. I called the number and mentioned the case number, just to find out that "I" took out a $500 loan from one of those cash stores (Fast Cash, Cash Express, Easy Cash ... I don't remember). After a couple years of nonpayment, with penalty and interest, it amounted to $2,300. They asked me how I would settle it; as soon as possible, they said, as a nonsettlement would affect our credit rating. The cash store was in Kansas City, Mo., a place that I've never set foot in. Just to prove that I was the person that I said I was, they sent me an affidavit asking for my history – both personal and financial. They asked for my driver license number, my bank accounts, my passport information, where I lived the past 10 years, and even the schools I attended. I took the information and went to the Milwaukee Police Department, but they claimed that they did not handle any identity theft cases.

After many sleepless nights, I finally settled with the credit company, proving that the person that took out the loan wasn't me. That was three years ago, and now it started all over again. I thought to myself, how many other innocent people are these companies threatening and intimidating with statements like: "This communication is from a debt collector. This is an attempt to collect a debt and any information obtained will be used for that purpose. As required by law, you are hereby notified that a negative credit report reflecting on your credit record may be submitted to a credit reporting agency if you fail to fulfill the terms of your credit obligations."

Identity theft has been around for a while and even movies were made about it. Fun when it happened to the movie characters, but not so funny when it happens to folks we know who ended up losing a fortune. There is a lot of information floating around and there are crooks sitting by desks figuring ways to create free and easy money. I talked to Erin Murphy, the chief of police in St. Croix Falls, just to find out that there are tons of scams out there, utilizing identity theft to take advantage of innocent citizens. Here are a few scams and what to do:

• **Grandparents scam** – elderly folks would get a call in the middle of the night. "Hi, grandma/grandpa, is that you?" If you answer, "Yes, Johnny, what's the matter?" the trap is set. Then "Johnny" would tell you that he is in jail, and needs help to get bail money. You'll be advised to go to Walmart a get $300 - $500 money order, and send to an account through Western Union. There is no trace once the money is sent and you just kiss it goodbye. Johnny would add, "Please don't tell Mom." Your money will never be seen again.

• **Lottery scam** – "You've just won the Jamaica Lottery. We need your bank account number so we can deposit your $250,000 winnings." And guess what will happen to the money you already have in your bank account. Or they'll ask you to prepay taxes and transferring fee to an account which cannot be traced.

• **Microsoft virus** – "To fix your problems, please pay whatever sum to this account or the virus will affect your computer, your bank account and all your personal information." Or, better yet, they'll give you a number to call, just to find out that there's a guy with an Indian accent answering, who is more than willing to help if you give him all your personal information.

• **IRS scam** – An IRS agent would call, just to let you know that the tax money that you owed is long due, and there would be a warrant for your arrest if the overdue amount is not settled in seven to 10 days.

• **Cloned cards** – Very popular in gas stations. There is a box with a miniature camera set next to the swipe machine to record your card number and passwords (called skimming). The crooks would make a duplicate card and use it to purchase merchandise or prepaid Visa cards and have a field day purchasing stuff until your account is depleted.

Advice from Chief Murphy:

• Ask questions – "What jail are you calling from, Johnny?"

Most jails have their address and phone numbers on the phone. If "Johnny" can't tell you, hang up. Or ask personal questions, like how many siblings do you have? Your parents name?

• The IRS scam is a common one and it is unlikely the IRS will call you. They will communicate with you through the mail. Hang up if IRS calls you.

• Call the local police about any suspicious calls.

• When you get calls from numbers that you don't recognize, simply hang up. Same with your emails. I have had calls that said, "If you want us to put you on a 'do not call list,' please press 1." Just to find out that I would have calls after calls soliciting their businesses for weeks after I press 1. It is their way to ask for permission to get in the door.

• No free lunch. Lottery winnings, or inheritance from the rich daughter from Kenya whose murdered father left her a fortune and wanted help to get the money out of the country and needs your bank account number to deposit the money.

"There are no ways to stop those crooks," Murphy said. "They will find new ways every day to take advantage of the innocent. Just be aware and be on alert. Report anything suspicious to the police. That's what we are here for."

Thanks, Chief, maybe we can all sleep a little better at night.

Computer virus

When we were living in Milwaukee, I made the mistake of downloading some "free" movies a friend told me about. The movies weren't any good to start with, but the troubles began. I started to have these sites appearing on my computer, prompting me to sign up for different services, games or programs in which I had no desire to participate. As in a miracle, a message popped up on my computer, and told me that my computer was infected by all these pop-up messages, and by calling the number they provided, they could help me "clean" my computer. Being a "computer dummy," I did call the number, and a guy with an Indian accent offered to help me fix my problems for free, yes, free. What a gentleman indeed. In order to clean my computer, he said he had to get inside my computer to find out where the virus is rooted. Having no sense of "common sense," I gave him my password, my code and whatever. So, the arrow on the screen went up and down for a few minutes. The problem was fixed, no more pop-ups, but little did I know that I just drank a cup of poison to quench my thirst. A few weeks later, a screen from F.B.I. popped up, stating that I was using my computer for some illegal activities, and the computer was blocked from further activities unless I paid a fine. I would have to go to get $350 money orders and send them to a special address. Till then, my computer was frozen, so to speak.

I took the computer to Best Buy, and they claimed that there was nothing they could do. Best to do then was to buy a new computer, and to download all the programs I already had; and just drop the old computer and move forward. I reluctantly did; and do you think I learned from that? Life has been good since moving up here to the North Woods, then trouble began again. No, I did not download any "free" movies or anything free. However, friends and families sent me emails and websites to read about certain messages, which I gladly obliged. Troubles began again when a screen kept popping up that said my computer was infected by a virus. I would be watching a movie on YouTube, and the screen would constantly be interrupted with different messages. The worst part came later with a warning message from Microsoft Technical Support, saying that my account was infected, and my personal data with any financial information or Social Security could easily be stolen. In order to protect my personal data, I should call a toll-free number. Mumbling, "Why me, why now?" I reluctantly called the number on the screen just to hear a guy with an Indian accent again, saying, "Aahlo, tis is George from Microsoft Technical Support, how can I help you." After I told "George" my problems, he said joyfully, "No problem, we can easily fix that for $99.95." The nightmare from Milwaukee surfaced immediately. "So George," I asked, "who do you work for?" I was curious. "Microsoft Technical Support, sir," he answered. "And just where is your office?" I persisted. "It is in Washington, sir." "What is the address, may I ask?" "Yes, 1668 South Washington Ave., sir." "Great," I said, "and what is the ZIP code?" "ZIP code, sir?" I could sense that he was puzzled. "Yes, the ZIP code of the state." Then he blurted out, "It is 92642, sir." I lived in California for a while, and their ZIP code starts with 9. Without wasting any more of my time, I just hung up on him.

With an infected computer, what to do? I still live in the Stone Age, and I use the computer for just a few functions – check my daily emails, Word for writing and Excel for composing charts. That's it! To not be able to use my computer would drive me crazy, it is like my connection with the outside world has been cut off. A good friend from the Leader (the local paper) suggested that I take the computer to the Easy I.T. Guys down the street from their downtown St. Croix Falls office and have them take a look see. I did, and I was most impressed with their expertise and their attitude on customer service.

I met with Josh, one of the technical support team, and he took the time time to let me know what the problems of my computers were, what I needed to do, and most important, what to do so it won't happen again. Again, living in the Stone Age, any information is great information. Here is a recap on his advice, thought you would be interested.

1) What kind of viruses are there in the market?

• Malware, Adware – they steal information from you. When you click onto an ad or check into an email with attachment, they can plant a program in your computer.

• Microsoft and pop-ups – they look legitimate, prompting you to call a certain number, just to suck you into their systems.

2) What do pop-ups do?

• They slow down your computer, create redirect – with web-pages and advertising.

• Steal information – either transfer your information or encrypt your information, through "free" movies or websites.

3) How to prevent/fix them?

• Do not download anything.

• Get an anti-virus program.

There are a lot of criminals sitting by the phone every day to find ways to take advantage of innocent folks. I had a gentleman who read my column told me that his mother was taken for a ride with the "Grandma, I am in jail and I need help" scheme. After grandma sent in the money to bail him out, a call from the "attorney" came right afterward and asked for more money. Grandma did, and guess what, she would never see her money or "grandson" again. Josh from the Easy I.T. Guys told me a lot about preventive maintenance on how to keep your computer safe and sound. It is just the peace of mind. I like what he said, " If you want to hire a bodyguard to protect you, would you hire someone who would dodge the bullet comes your way, or someone who would actually take the bullet for you?" I like that.

Yes, I know that he'll take the bullet for me.

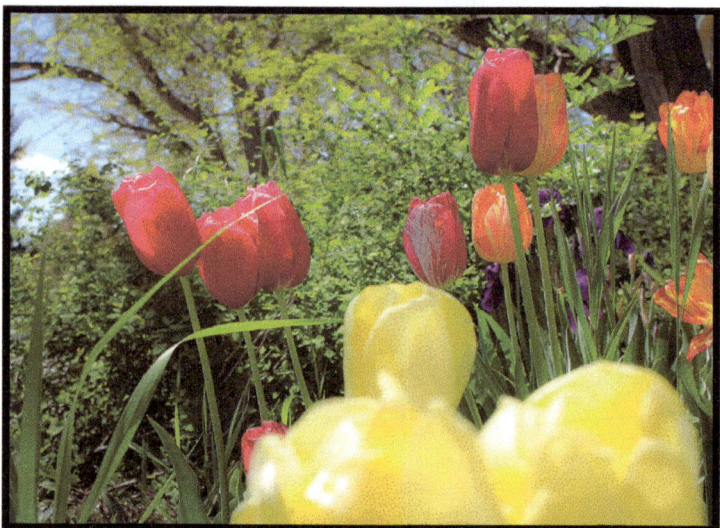

CHAPTER TEN: GARDENING

The joy of gardening

My wife started a small garden in early spring with the help of many of our friends and neighbors. I totally stayed out of it, as I am still in the "city boy" mode. Growing up in the cement forest in Hong Kong, I knew nothing about gardening. She really takes it seriously, and I do have tremendous respect for the hard work she put in. First, she built a fence around her garden with posts and a swinging gate and then the planter boxes which are gopher-proof. Living in an area where animals roam freely, she has to do a lot of extra work to make sure that the squirrels, gophers and deer do not enjoy the fruits, or vegetables, of her labor easily.

The first few months were OK, with some snow peas, carrots and radishes to munch on. Then, all of a sudden, she started to bring in squash, zucchinis and cucumbers in buckets. And on top of that, our neighbors and friends are doing same. They are taking up all the precious spaces for my beer in the fridge, and I have to do something. What better way than to eat them and get rid of them. I heard a story that folks used to leave baskets of zucchinis and cucumbers at their neighbors' house at midnight and sneak away. May be I'll try that soon. But meanwhile, I've found ways to get rid of them. Here are some simple recipes:

Quickie pickie pickle *(makes 6 quarts with 12 cucumbers) 6-8 cucumbers, sliced paper thin*
> 2 cups wine vinegar
> 2 cups water
> 2 cups sugar
> 2 tablespoons kosher salt
> 4 cloves garlic, peeled and smashed
> 1/8 teaspoon red pepper flakes, optional

Boil the wine vinegar, water, sugar, salt, garlic and red pepper flakes first; adjust the seasoning to taste. The red pepper flakes definitely add a kick. Add the sliced cucumbers and store in the refrigerator. It can keep for four to six weeks. Great with salads or your burger.

What to do with all those zucchinis? I have two recipes for them. One is just to stir-fry them with onions and mushrooms, and another is to make a zucchini pie (quiche) with brats or Italian sausage.

Stir-fried zucchini mix
3 zucchinis, sliced thin
1 yellow squash, sliced thin 1 tomato, quartered
1 red onion, sliced thin

In a heated frying pan, add oil and two cloves smashed garlic. Add red onion, tomatoes, squash and zucchini. Stir-fry for three to four minutes. Add 2-3 ounces of wine (red or white, doesn't matter). Make sure the chef shares some. Put lid on and let it cook for one to two more minutes. Add 1/8 teaspoon of kosher salt and some ground pepper. It is unbelievable! Be creative, add whatever you find in your garden – string beans, Brussels sprouts, carrots and some button mushrooms; the list can go on and on. Simple pleasure at its best.

Remember the joke I posted earlier? That a gentleman ordered a "quickie" in a cafe and got slapped by the waitress? Well, here it is, the quickie quiche.

Quickie quiche *(makes two pies)* 2 *pie crusts (Pillsbury)*
8 eggs
4 cups grated cheese
1 can condensed milk
1 pound sausage mix, chopped and cooked
2 zucchinis, shredded and cooked
2 cups sliced mushrooms, 1 cup for each pie

Turn oven on to 400 F. Unroll the pie crusts and place in two oiled glass pie dishes. Bake in oven for 15-20 minutes till brown. Take them out of the oven and layer the zucchini, sausage and mushrooms in the crusts. Mix eggs, cheese and milk and pour over pies. Turn oven down to 375 F and let them cook for 20-30 minutes. They are done when a toothpick doesn't stick to the ingredients. The top will be golden brown and puffed up. Let them cool off and enjoy.

It is a lot of work to make the quiche, so I usually make two at a time, one for the road, and one for the freezer.

Have you found ways to get rid of your tomatoes yet? Make tomato salad, grill them and top with cheese, make salsa (pico de gallo), marinate them and serve them on grilled toast. Make your own V-8. The list can go on and on. Enjoy your garden, and enjoy summer.

Garden explosion

A few days ago, Paul, my good friend and neighbor down the street, came over with some boxes of vegetables from his garden. "Can you take these, please?" I could see the tears in his eyes. "We have so many vegetables in our garden that we don't know what to do with them. Our neighbors won't even answer the door when they see my truck pull up, knowing that I will have boxes of vegetables to offer them." Oh, what a happy problem. "Of course I will take them. Yes, all of them," I said.

I was amazed to see what came out of his garden. There were purple string beans, onions, lettuce mix, cucumbers and many more. Goodness, it could feed a commune. I definitely could use those products in my cooking classes. So, instead of beef and broccoli, could we do beef and garden string beans? And what about the onions? The zucchini? The cucumbers? The tomatoes? Oh, life is good, there are so many things to do with what the good earth provides. This is going to be a great summer after all.

Let's start with the cucumbers. I made a cucumber salad with sesame dressing earlier and it was a hit. I'm going to share it with you here.

Cucumber salad with sesame dressing
Ingredients:
Cucumbers, 6 each, thinly sliced.
Tomatoes, 1 each, core removed, finely chopped.
Scallions, 3 stalks, finely chopped or sliced.
Dressing ingredients:
Olive oil, 1/4 cup.
Sesame oil, 2 tablespoons.
Soy sauce, 1 cup.
Vinegar, apple cider or regular, 1 cup.
Garlic, 2 cloves, finely minced.
Salt, 1/2 teaspoon.
Brown sugar, 1/2 tablespoon.
Red pepper flakes, 1/2 teaspoon.

Sesame seeds, 1 tablespoon.
Red wine, 1/2 cup (and another half cup for the chef).

Adjust the flavor to your liking by adding more sugar if you like it sweeter or more vinegar if you prefer a more sour flavor. Mix salad dressing well, pour onto the cucumber mix and marinate for at least one hour before serving. Top with sesame seeds before serving. Add a pinch of red pepper chili for coloring and extra flavor.

Zucchini, zucchini and more zucchini

Last year, we had more zucchini than we knew what to do with. It seemed like every time we harvested a mutant zucchini from our garden, another one would pop up overnight. While my wife was overjoyed at her hard work in planting them, I was busy creating recipes to get rid of them. Goodness, we could only eat so much of it. While fresh is best, I have found ways to preserve them for the cold winter season. Making zucchini bread is one way, as once it is made, it can be kept in the freezer for six months to a year.

We will definitely try them this year as we finally decided to get a larger refrigerator. It is over 60 percent larger than our old one and literally saved our marriage! Our old one came with the house. It was adequate for a small family. However, with my cooking classes, the tiny fridge just didn't have enough space. My wife couldn't find the food she wanted, as it would be hidden behind all my prepped food for the classes. Then, I would be mad that the leftovers were spoiled. But who's to blame? They were well hidden behind stuff for my classes. Yes, life is complicated. Then came this new refrigerator and life is good. The left side is reserved for her stuff and the right side is mine. No crossing the line and no blaming each other. It is peace and harmony. Why didn't we think of it earlier?

Oh, sorry, totally forgot about the zucchini business. So, what to do when my wife brings in three or four oversized zucchinis with a big smile on her face every day. Yes, every day, three or four oversized zucchinis. Don't they sleep at night?

Being creative, my first thought was how to get rid of them in a nice way. Here are some ways to start. Trust me, you can come up with more recipes yourself. In the meantime, try the below.

Zucchini stir-fry
If you have a large family, this is a perfect recipe to feed 8-10 people. If you have a small family, two to four people, it might last a week. So, I'll just provide the standard recipe and you folks can adjust accordingly.

Ingredients:
Zucchini, 1 oversize, 2-4 lbs., sliced to bite size.
Onion, 1 each, sliced.
Tomatoes, 1 each, quartered.
Black bean sauce, 1 teaspoon.
Oyster sauce, 1 tablespoon.
In a heated wok or saute pan, add 1 tablespoon oil, then black bean sauce. Add all ingredients and cook until tender. Add some wine to steam up the vegetables. Don't forget, half of the wine goes to the chef and the other to the food. The final touch is the oyster sauce and voila! This recipe could be used to create a veggie burger or pasta salad, too.

Now, for the tomatoes. Yes, as much as we love them, it can be a nightmare when you have too many. What to do?

Well, I like to make Pico de Gallo. Do you remember what that is? Then, stewed tomatoes, with same recipe from the cucumber salad, and tomato soup, either steamed and creamy or chilled. Or how about bruschetta, pronounced bro-ska-ta, for an Italian dinner? Actually, the same one recipe can apply to many entrees. You just have to be creative.

Here are the recipes for Pico de Gallo, which translates to beak of the rooster, and bruschetta. But don't ever pronounce it as bro-shet-ta to an Italian, unless you're ready to get yelled at. I learned my lesson.

Pico de Gallo

Ingredients:

    Tomatoes, 6 each.

    Celery, 1 stalk, diced.

    Red onion, 1/2 each, diced.

    Jalapenos, 1/2 each, diced and seeded.

    Cilantro, 1/2 cup, finely chopped.

    Salt, 1 teaspoon.

    Lime juice, 1 each.

Bruschetta

    Ingredients:

    Tomatoes, 6 each, diced and cored.

    Celery, 1 stalk, diced.

    Red onion, 1/2 each, diced.

    Green pepper, 1/2 each, diced and seeded.

    Italian parsley, 1/2 cup, finely chopped.

    Salt, 1 teaspoon.

    Lemon juice, 1 each.

    Italian dressing, 1/2 cup.

Well, there you go, same ingredients but with a twist. You have two different specials to wow your guests. Pico de Gallo is best to serve with tortilla chips and margaritas, while bruschetta is best served on toasted Italian bread slices with a glass of chianti.

Life is good, no!?

War in movies and reality

Oh, how I loved war movies when I was a kid growing up in Hong Kong. John Wayne was my hero. No matter who he fought, he always kicked their behinds – the Indians, the Germans and the Japanese. Well, he was outnumbered in the Alamo, but who's to blame? I loved watching the soldiers marching in uniform, it always gave me a thrill. To watch all those fancy, powerful and sophisticated weapons taking out the enemies, wished I was old enough to use them. The Japanese invasion was still fresh in my mind.

They occupied China for eight years, and were in Hong Kong for three years and eight months. While slaughtering thousands to show their sovereign power, they never apologized or addressed those issues. "What?" they would tell the world, "those things never happened." They literally erased the killings from the textbooks. "Comfort women, never happened." "Using live people to experiment warfare weapons? There is no proof." "Nanking Massacre, who witnessed it?" Yet, the actors in Hollywood movies would show a sad face and exclaim, "Yes, I keep this watch my father left me. He was killed in Hiroshima." Sorry, buddy, but why was the bomb dropped in the first place?

Enough of that. I loved John Wayne, growing up, and watching young Eddie Murphy wiping out the whole German unit firing from a burning tank was mesmerizing. Not to mention Captain York, who captured hundreds of enemies with just a few of his fellow soldiers. What heroes indeed. I used to love watching the gunfire from the Navy ships, how powerful! The rockets that hit the shores and blew up all the barracks. Wow, wow, wow. I watched "The Longest Day" when I was 10 or 12 years old. Just watching all the soldiers in action gave me the chills. Thousands and thousands of men would fight the enemy from land, air and sea. What a glorious battle, to fight, protect, defend and to gain back what freedom meant to be. I have watched "The

Longest Day" a thousand times, while loving all the action –
the bombings, troops jumping off the airplanes and the rat-a-
tat of machine guns. It was exciting for a young kid, thinking
that war is fun.

Coming to the states, my first encounter with war was at a
cafe in Oceanside, Calif. I was playing guitar in a small cafe
downtown. Then I saw an elderly gentleman who wanted
to play a song with my guitar. He sang, and I was touched
by his voice and his fancy guitaring. "Wow, that was great,"
I exclaimed. He looked at me and asked warmly, "How old
do you think I am?" Based on his look and his mannerism, I
said, "Sir, 30, may be a bit older?" Then he grabbed my hand,
and said, "Brother, I am your age, I guess around 20? Been to
Vietnam for a year, and that's what war does to you." I was
speechless. Just what do you mean by that? He left before I
could ask more questions. But my image of a glorious war
had dimmed.

My dad is a Marine, even though he has retired, but once a
Marine, you'll always be a Marine. Thank goodness he was
a mechanic and never engaged in battle. But I remember
that he would be gone for months at a time for duties, and I
would be left in charge of all the household duties, making
sure that my siblings did theirs. It wasn't until my wife and
I got married that I faced the reality of war a bit more. Both
of my brother- in-law were engaged in battle duties. Tony,
my older brother- in-law, was in Vietnam. He was shot three
times and is still happy to tell his stories every time we get
together. What a brave soul, doing what you think is right
for your fellowman and your country. How dare I complain
when I cut my finger prepping for a cooking class? Another
brother-in-law, Darryl, was stationed in Iraq for a while.
He was the one who, upon his return from his deployment,
tasted my food that I made for him and wanted to marry me.

My view of the war has turned, slowly but surely. It is not
glorious anymore, it is hell and it is real! The bullets are real,
the bomb blasts are real and the killings are just as real.

I watched Steven Spielberg's "Saving Private Ryan" the
first time, and I was horrified. Soldiers would be killed before
they even got off their boats. The scene with the soldiers

drowning in their gear, the limbs getting blown off and the shots coming every which way while they all tried to surface for air. My goodness, I was crying the whole time. What would I do in such circumstances? Would I still go to war and join others, knowing that all these things could happen to me? Yet, hundreds and thousands went with no second thoughts. They wanted to serve, to protect and to defend the innocent. What a price to pay, to sacrifice your own life, leaving your dearest family behind, just to do what is right!

I watch YouTube before I go to bed, a dumb movie here and there and some comedy shows. I stumbled across some clips on "The Surprise Visits of the Troops," where they show soldiers from different units coming home to surprise their families – in classrooms, at a baseball game, at a restaurant, or whatever. The expressions on everyone's faces were priceless. That's what you look like before a heart attack – your eyes light up, your mouth drops, then you let up the loudest scream and then on to the person with your dear life.

I watched little girls/boys in school screaming and crying; wives and parents in restaurants; kids engaging in a game and seeing their parents strolled in. How can one not hold back the tears?

I used to travel a lot, two to three weeks at a time. But these compadres of ours, they are deployed months at a time, not being able to spend any quality time with their families. It is indeed a sacrifice that is above and beyond any responsibilities. To all those that are out there serving our country, many thanks. Somehow, watching war movies ain't the same anymore. Yes, there's a new meaning. Thank you all out there for taking care of us.

New New Year

Just how much worries and troubles are there? Giving birth, getting old, feeling sick and dying. We are all surrounded by emotions – happy, angry, sad and contented. But everything is just a moment's sentiment. So, what's one living for? What's the purpose of survival? Working from 9 to 5 just to raise our children? To work your whole life and to end up with what? At the very end, what's the difference between a multi-billionaire and a penniless beggar? We all ended up being a corpse buried 6' under.

So, working hard our whole life for fame and fortune, is it what our life is about? And look at all these emperors and kings throughout history. To be the ruler and conqueror of a continent wasn't enough, they had to rule the world. How many lives were lost, how many families were separated with broken homes. All because of one person's selfishness and greed. The history repeated over and over for the past 4,000 years. When will there be peace? And when will the people ever have a taste of harmony and tranquility?

Looking at the stars at night, there are immeasurable. There are countless galaxies with numerous planets. We as mankind are so proud of the pyramids and The Great Wall. But all that's only about 2,000 to 3,000 years of history. Even the earth itself is only about 4 1/2 billion years old. Compare to 4 1/2 billion, 4,000 is a minute number. And a lot of scientists told us there are many, many other galaxies which are billions and billions of light years away. So, what is the big deal about these light years?

Well, our day consists of a second, a minute, an hour and then a day, a week, a month and then a year. The speed of light can travel 186,000 mile in a second. To circle the earth once, it is only 24,900 miles. In a sense, in a second, the speed of light can circle the earth 7.5 times. There are 60 seconds in a minute, 60 minutes in an hour, and 24 hours in a day. So, there are 86,400 seconds in a day. And with 365 days in a year, the speed of light can travel 5,865,696,000,000 miles. (Don't try this with your calculator, it goes ERROR after the fourth try).

A lot of stars that we can see today do not exist anymore. They exploded millions and millions of years ago, and it took that long to reach our eyes on earth. I started to understand now that the past, the present and the future can all exist in the same space. And just how small our planet is, comparing to all these other larger and older cosmos from different galaxies? And in that token, just how trivial and insignificant is my existence? My being here or not being here is totally irrelevant. If we keep worrying about our own existence, our possession, and all our belongings, that's how troubles begin; as we will worry sick about keeping or losing them. But, what if we step back and stop worrying, as all these possessions have no meaning at all. What if I don't exist anymore? What if the existence or others are more important? Something to think about.

My wife and I were having dinner at a lovely's couple home, and as they were showing us the pictures of their family – present and past. All so wonderful. Then the topic came up, what would you salvage if your house is on fire? It is a tough topic indeed. What are your most precious possession in your life time? The pictures of your ancestors? The China set from great grandma? The quilt that grandma made when you were 2 years old? All these treasures are priceless. You can't simply put a price tag on it. And that hits me – you can't put a price tag on it. We're surrounded by materialistic stuff our whole life. How much that mansion costs? And why would you need 8 to 10 of those mansions with 50 rooms when you only need one bedroom to sleep in? And those fancy cars? When all we need is only one trustworthy car to get us to the destination and back, why someone would have a fleet of antique cars, each worth millions of dollars, just idling in their garage? No, don't know the answer, and don't care to find out. For some folks, the more you get, the more you want. But for what purposes?

Many folks have spent their life time acquiring what they think would make them happy – a big huge mansion (in different parts of the world), expensive automobiles, diamonds and jewelries, and artworks or artifacts. So, they have gathered more and more, and then more and more. But, are they happy?

It is hard to define happiness, as I do not possess any of the 'basic requirements' for happiness.' No, no big mansion. We live in a small log cabin facing the lake, able to watch sunrise each morning at the front porch, and sunrise each evening at the back porch; with the marching through of a parade of wild turkeys occasionally as a bonus. And no fancy cars in the garage. I have a leased car and my wife's Honda Fit is 'old.'

And we don't have a garage to speak of, as it has turned to be her studio of art creations. My wife, Colleen, is an artist, she can paint, make jewelries, does potteries and whatever. Thank goodness she can't cook. Otherwise she won't need me.

We found happiness through friendship, love, caring and giving; and be able to do what you enjoy most in life. Life is not about counting coins at night about how much you have generated, but about the love you've generated of how much you have given and received in return.

Understanding that what we observe doesn't exist anymore open my eyes. If you do not have any possessions, then what do you worry about? If we all put others well-being ahead of our own, then hopefully our world will be a more peaceful one. Right? Happy New Year to you all.

"Twinkle, twinkle Little Stars"

We have moved to the countryside since last June. Needless to say, my wife and I enjoy our new lifestyle immensely. It is just so peaceful and quiet, and folks are so open, warm and friendly. I love the mornings - sipping my tea in the back porch, listening to the rustling leaves and watching the birds gliding over my head. And sunsets are simply spectacular. It is a different show every evening. I never knew that there are so many different colors, and just how beautiful it can be when they are all blended together. Then, as soon as the sunset curtain closes, another show begins.

Living in the cities, I have never seen so many stars before, ever. It is mind-boggling – just how many stars are twinkling out there? And how many of them are looking back at us with a smile? Just then, while I was wondering these things, I received an email from an old friend. The title is "Earth in True Perspective" (you can Google it). And it answers all my questions. When we lived in Milwaukee, anywhere that required more than 20 minutes' drive was considered "long distance." And here, any place that requires over an hour drive is fair game. Everything is relative.

Our solar system consists of Earth, Mars, Mercury, Venus, Uranus, Jupiter, Neptune and Saturn; all orbiting around the sun. Comparing to the sun, Earth is the size of a sesame seed. But then, there are other stars which are even bigger and larger than the sun. Can you imagine that? There are Sirius, Pollux, Arcturus, Rigil, Aldebaran, Betelgeuse, Eta Carinae, and plenty others, each one much bigger and brighter than our own sun. And scientists keep discovering new stars or planets which are millions and millions of light years away. Hmm, I thought to myself, 1 million is a pretty large number (there are six zeros). 100 million will be 100,000,000. It is a big number indeed. But then, how far is the distance of a light year? I did a little research, and find out that a light year is how far the light can travel in a year. Well, there are 60 seconds in a minute, 60 minutes in an hour, 24 hours in a day, and 365 days in a year. So, in a sense, there are 60 X 60 X 24 X 365 seconds, or 31 million seconds in a year. Well, 31,536,000 seconds to be exact. And just how far does light travel in a second?

To go around the equator, there's roughly 25,000 miles. And, in one second, the speed of light can travel around the earth about 7.5 times. Yes, 7.5 times! That's about 187,500 miles that light can travel in just one second. Unbelievable to comprehend, isn't it? One blink of an eye, and the light can travel all that distance. Well, there are 31 million seconds in a year. So, 31,000,000 seconds times 187,500 miles equals the distance that light can travel in one year. That's roughly 5,797,000,000,000 miles that light can travel in one year. And just how many times we can go around the earth? Now, with these newfound planets 30 million light years away, just how far away is that? Well, 5,797,000,000 X 30,000,000, or 173,910,000,000,000,000. It is just bunch of zeros. When we hear the government tell us that we are running $250 trillion deficit, it is just bunch of zeros.

OK, are you ready for more exciting news? On March 9, 2003, the Hubble Space Telescope noticed a bright little star which is 1/10 the size of the moon. So, for four months, the telescope just zeroed in on the same spot and took pictures.

And the result was overwhelming! That little spot actually was a picture consisting of more than 1,000,000,000 (1 trillion) stars; and each star has more than 10,000 galaxies. And that's only off one single dot in the sky! So, how many stars/ planets/galaxies are there in the sky? An old quote from our famous astrologer Carl Sagan, there are "Billions and billions" out there. Some of the stars are so old that they already exploded billions of years ago and no longer exist. But it is not till now that the light actually reaches our naked eye. It is mind-boggling knowing that the past, the present, and the future can stand still at the same moment.

So, million, billion, and trillion, what's the difference? I did some more research, and found out that:

1 million (1,000,000) seconds = 13 days
1 billion (1,000,000,000) seconds = 31 years

MY PHILOSOPHY OF LIFE

1 trillion (1,000,000,000,000) seconds = 31,688 years
To be politically correct, when I sing the nighttime lullaby to my granddaughter, I guess I have to change the lyrics:
"Twinkle twinkle giant stars
I'll never know how many there are
Up above so far and high
Many galaxies in the sky
Twinkle twinkle giant stars
I'll never know how many there are."
I'll never complain how far I have to drive ever again. What is 500 miles comparing to 5,797,000,000,000 miles?

So much to learn, part 1

A few months ago, I got an email from my barbershop buddy Ken Gonske. He sings right next to me in the chorus, but a different part. I sing lead and he sings tenor, which is the higher pitched part. Anyway, he was helping his grandson raise money for a project which I found intriguing, to build shelters for the homeless in Guatemala. Many questions came to my mind including, what, why and how in the world would he be able to do that? So, I asked Ken in our next practice just what this was about. Then he told me that James Ronaldo Meyer is his adopted grandson from Guatemala. He came to this country when he was a 1-year-old. He never forgets his roots. With his parents' encouragement, his dream is to raise money so the folks back home can have a better life, whether it be having some pigs or chickens to raise at their homes, or better yet, to have a place they can actually call home.

"That's a big dream," I thought to myself.

So I called Ken and asked him how much money his grandson was thinking to raise. "$10,000," he said.

"What, is this kid out of his mind, raising $10,000 for people that live in places that we have no idea where it even is?" I asked.

"Yup," Ken said, "That's what James would like to do, and we'll do what we can to help." That was four or five months ago.

I did some consulting work in Guatemala 10 to 15 years ago. It is a beautiful country, yet kind of disturbing in many ways. While the rich are very rich, the poor are very poor. I was there to help a company starting a new restaurant concept. Yes, the owner wanted to serve Chinese cuisine to the Guatemalans. So, my challenge was to create recipes and to teach the locals to cook Chinese food.

It was a challenge indeed. But we did start the business with a big bang. Folks just love it.

I was in the city of Guatemala for about a month. A

beautiful country indeed, with a lot of interesting history. I didn't have time to visit all the ancient sites with pyramids and statues from the Inca Empire. I spent a lot of time visiting the local marketplaces searching for the right ingredients for the recipes. I never forgot about the sight of the local dump where people dumped their trash, ready to be picked up later by the city officials. The trash included the waste from local merchants and included vegetables, fruits and meat. The sight of 40 or 50 kids, aged 3 to 10, salvaging the waste and searching for food just broke my heart. And I thought I had a rough childhood!

Another interesting thing that I noticed was that every place I went, there would be a guard bearing a shotgun in the front, whether it was a restaurant, a bank, a grocery store, any business. I stayed at a hotel and just across the street was a primary school for kids aged 6 to 10. I couldn't help but notice that every morning, two limousines would pull up and five or six bodyguards would accompany one young child into the school. "Must be a rich kid!" I thought. Then I was told that the rebels would kidnap folks in broad daylight. I laughed at the silly thought, until I heard what I thought were firecrackers going off outside one morning. It was when the front-desk clerk told me that it was actually a machine gun from the guerrillas that I decided it was time to leave. I left that afternoon and have never set foot again in Guatemala. Then here comes James with his dreams.

I told Ken that I would love to help his grandson James with his dreams, but money, I have none.

"However," I said, "I could donate my cooking service to help. I have done that many times in the past, to do a cooking demonstration at their homes, and to sing a few songs with my guitar afterwards."

Ken took my idea and came back a few weeks later with a smile, saying, "Yes, Peter, you're on. We've raised $500 for you to cook for us." And so I did, for the family of 18. What a joy indeed, to help a young boy fulfill his dream.

A few weeks later, I asked Ken about the progress of his grandson's project, how he was doing with his goal of raising $10,000. "Oh, he did well. He has raised $17,000 for his project," he told me.

What? I thought to myself, a 10-year-old kid raised $17,000 on his own? I needed to find out for my own sake. I had no idea what I was doing when I was 10 years old, and now this kid raised $17,000 to help others? How did he do it?

I arranged a meeting with him and his mom, Arlaina Meyer, and learned so much more about how his dreams unfolded. A really touching story indeed. It all started out when James was brushing his teeth and left the water running. His mom told him to turn the water off, as it is a waste of water usage when thousands could use it, especially in Guatemala, where he is from. James was adopted when he was 1 year old. His birth mother gave him up for adoption as she couldn't raise him the way she wanted with her mere wages, with so many other mouths to feed. So, Arlaina and Damon Meyers adopted him with help from the Faith in God's Mission agency and a beautiful relationship began.

James' first goal was to get a water pump for a family in need in Guatemala, so they could get fresh drinking water. It would take $285 to get a pump and James started his own fundraising. Instead of bringing gifts to his birthday party, he asked his friends to bring coins. They all did and the water pump was installed in his honor.

So much to learn, part 2

For years Damon and Arlaina Meyer prayed for a family. Recognizing their pain, Arlaina's sister Allison shared a news clipping advertising an adoption informational meeting. When Arlaina entered the meeting room, the director of the adoption agency was in the front of the room with her head bowed in prayer asking that someone would come to give a home to a little one in Guatemala who so desperately needed one. Nine months later, Damon and Arlaina tucked in a small 1-year-old boy and shared a bedtime story that would be repeated over and over again. "Once upon a time there was a little boy named James Ronaldo Meyer. His mommy and daddy loved him so much that they traveled far, far away to another country to bring him home. He is their gift from God and his life will bring God glory."

Since 2012, James Ronaldo's classmates from St. Joseph Catholic School in Rice Lake have come together for a play date for his birthday each year. Instead of presents, they brought coins, and throughout the years those coins filled and overflowed several glass pitchers. The outpouring of generosity from these little ones and James' extended family enabled the purchase of water pumps, chicks, piglets and goats for families in need in Guatemala through an organization called Food for the Poor, foodforthepoor.org. Food for the Poor, based out of Coconut Creek, Fla., helps provide food, housing, clean water, education, emergency relief and more to help fight poverty in 17 countries in the Caribbean and Latin America.

In 2016 James turned 10 years old. For his golden birthday, his parents shared that they would be taking a mission trip to Guatemala with Food for the Poor. Upon returning from Guatemala, the Meyer Family was determined to do something to help share God's love with their brothers and sisters in Guatemala. But what? With the faith of a child, James decided that he wanted two new homes built in Guatemala for families that so desperately needed adequate shelter. Food for the Poor helped the Meyer Family establish a Champions for the Poor site, foodforthepoor. org/jamesronaldo, to assist others in contributing towards James' goal through online giving. A total of $14,400 would be needed to build the two double-unit homes and James had decided that he wanted to accomplish his goal by the end of 2016, giving him just over one month to achieve it.

James had $6 to give and $14,394 to go. Thanks to Wisconsin winters, he earned a bit more shoveling snow for a friend from church, but he definitely needed help. James had "set a goal so high that unless God was involved it would have been impossible." His Grandpa Gonske, known for his positive attitude, was not afraid to share his grandson's goal with everyone he could. Aunt Amber asked James to be a guest on her WJMC radio program. Normally this shy young man would have passed on the offer, but God gave him the strength to share his passion with others. He mustered up the courage to speak to church members at Bethany Lutheran and then at Our Lady of Lourdes Catholic Church. Friends and family put together a chili supper and Peter Kwong shared his talents by cooking for an additional fundraiser meal. Family, friends, churches, businesses and even those he had yet to meet stood behind him with gifts of prayers, encouragement and financial support.

On New Year's Eve, the Meyer family gathered with friends in a church group called Anchored in Christ. James was just $250 away from reaching his goal. Before midnight, a donation for $250 came in with the message "James! You reached your goal! God brought all of us together to help build houses because of you. God used you and your giving and caring heart to work miracles! His love is extravagant."

To date, $17,000 has been raised. Eight months later, two families in El Durazno, Amatitlan, Guatemala, are sheltered by new homes. James is gearing up for sixth grade and loves playing piano, drawing, hanging out with his cousin and having water balloon fights with his 5å-year-old little sister, Elliot Rose. He dreams of becoming an agriculture teacher someday and traveling back to Guatemala to meet those who have touched his life. He's only $4,600 away from a third house being funded and would love to see another family sheltered. Once again, it's a big goal, but with God's help he knows it's possible.

The Meyer Family is composed of a dad, mom, son and daughter. All were born in different places with different last names. Through tears of struggles and joy, God brought their family together through the gift of adoption. Through the gift of adoption, we are all able to be part of God's family. We may have different genetics, backgrounds and talents, but when we share love and our gifts with others, we bring God glory!

AFTERWARD

Impossible Dreams are possible, if you just keep believing with your heart! So far, I'm counting all my blessings of how many impossible dreams I have achieved because of my believing; and of course, thanks to my lucky stars above. Coming from Hong Kong as a foreign student, my American host family legally adopted me so I could become an American citizen. Hence my legal name of Peter House Kwong. So many impossible dreams followed afterwards.

I've moved around the country many times with my family. Starting from San Diego, California, we moved to Arlington, Texas. Then to Atlanta, Georgia; and finally to Milwaukee, Wisconsin. My wife and I ended up in the North Woods in Wisconsin, which I know is going to be our final destination. This is home, the end of the rainbow.

Not knowing anyone up here and not knowing what to do were the biggest fears before the move. Somehow, my lucky stars kept shining on me. I've found so many friends singing with the Indianhead barbershop chorus; and got invited to write a column at the Inter-County Leader. Also, with all the cooking classes in different counties, I've become a local celebrity. Folks would recognize me at the bank, grocery stores or coffee shops. Never expected all that in a million years.

When Gary King, the editor of Inter-County Leader approached me about putting all the articles that I've written in the 'Wok & Roll' column into a book, I thought he was kidding. But then again, my life has been filled with impossible dreams; so why not? I've improved a lot of my writing skills since I started writing the column. Now approaching the final stage of my cookbook, I feel quite confident of how I compose the story of growing up in Hong Kong and starting a new life in the States. At first, the name of the cook book was named "Cook with your heart"; then I thought "Cook from your heart" was a better choice. Then one day, it dawned on me that while I was growing up, we greeted each other with "Have you eaten?" instead of "Good morning, how are you?" As food was scarce in the old days, it was a blessing that you have a full stomach. So, "Have you eaten?" would become the title of my memoir/cookbook.

Thanks to everyone who gives me the encouragement to keep writing. Thanks to those who attended my cooking classes and gave me praises. Most of all, thanks to those who believe in me – my wife Colleen, Gary King the editor; and finally, my American mom and dad – Joyce and Donald House. Without them, all these dreams would not be possible.